Toward a General Theory of Organizing – Volume 1: Introducing the Network Field Model

Authored by Steef Peters and Karen Stephenson

Published in London, United Kingdom

Toward a General Theory of Organizing - Volume 1: Introducing the Network Field Model
http://dx.doi.org/10.5772/intechopen.99709
Authored by Steef Peters and Karen Stephenson

First published in London, United Kingdom, 2022 by IntechOpen
IntechOpen is the global imprint of INTECHOPEN LIMITED, registered in England and Wales, registration number: 11086078, 5 Princes Gate Court, London, SW7 2QJ, United Kingdom

British Library Cataloguing-in-Publication Data
A catalogue record for this book is available from the British Library

Additional hard and PDF copies can be obtained from orders@intechopen.com

Toward a General Theory of Organizing - Volume 1: Introducing the Network Field Model
Authored by Steef Peters and Karen Stephenson
p. cm.
Print ISBN 978-1-80355-141-8
Online ISBN 978-1-80355-142-5
eBook (PDF) ISBN 978-1-80355-143-2

Meet the authors

After a joint liberal arts degree in quantum chemistry and art, Karen Stephenson went on to earn a master's in Mathematical Modeling in Anthropology at the University of Utah where she worked with the mathematician Frank Harary deciphering patterns in ancient trade networks followed by a Ph.D. in Anthropology at Harvard University where she worked with statistician Marvin Zelen in exposing network patterns in the infamous AIDS network surrounding Patient Zero. While serving time as a professor of management at the Anderson School of Management at UCLA, she started her own company NetForm with the encouragement and support of IBM. In that decade, she developed three software products containing algorithms for identifying repeating patterns in human networks in businesses, universities, governments and economic regions. Her work has been featured by Malcolm Gladwell in the New Yorker along with features in The Economist, Forbes, CIO, Wired, WSJ and many other outlets. She is the recipient of numerous awards for innovation during her career. Presently she is partnering with Peters to apply her algorithms in wallet79. Currently, she is teaching at the School of Management (SOM) at Yale University and the Erasmus Center for Women and Organizations (ECWO) at the Rotterdam School of Management.

After studying mathematics and physics at the University of Amsterdam and a Ph.D. in Elementary Particle Physics, Steef Peters stepped outside of academia to design and implement an electronic payment system and develop artificial intelligence applications in the financial sector. This resulted in a professorship at the Free University of Amsterdam, visiting researcher position at the Henley Business School, and visiting professor position at the Beijing Institute of Technology. Afterward, he started companies in the Netherlands and the Philippines focused on the design and implementation of decentralized personal information systems. In order to apply this knowledge, he joined a social domain company as a director, resulting in a talent identification and matching model that is now being developed in a new company, wallet79. Currently, he is teaching at the Hague University of Applied Sciences in the field of risk management, cybersecurity, blockchain and GDPR.

Toward a General Theory of Organizing

Volume 1: Introducing the Network Field Model

Volume 2: Applying the Network Field Model
Volume 3: Using the Network Field Model

S. Peters
K. Stephenson

Published in London, United Kingdom

Table of Contents

Toward a General Theory of Organizing – Volume 1: Introducing the Network Field Model

Steef Peters and Karen Stephenson

Abstract

There are three volumes in this body of work. In volume one, we lay the foundation for a general theory of organizing. We propose that organizing is a continuous process of ongoing mutual or reciprocal influence between objects (e.g., human actors) in a field, whereby a field is infinite and connects all the objects in it much like electromagnetic fields influence atomic and molecular charged objects or gravity fields influence inanimate objects with mass such as planets and stars. We use field theory to build what we now call the Network Field Model. In this model, human actors are modeled as point-like objects in the field. Influence *between* and investments *in* these point-like human objects are explained as energy exchanges (potential and kinetic) which can be described in terms of three different types of *capital*: financial (assets), human capital (the individual) and social (two or more humans in a network). This model is predicated on a field theoretical understanding about the world we live in. We use historical and contemporaneous examples of human activity and describe them in terms of the model. In volume two, we demonstrate how to apply the model. In volume 3, we use experimental data to prove the reliability of the model. These three volumes will persistently challenge the reader's understanding of time, position and what it means to be part of an infinite field.

Keywords: network, field theory, financial capital, human capital, social capital

1. Introduction

Moving
in a field
feels like
building
my existence
again and again;
finding
my way with
the others
around me;
setting new values
together.

The reader is now in volume one, where the authors build the foundation for a general theory of organizing. Organizing is a continuous process of ongoing mutual or reciprocal influence between objects (e.g., human actors) in a field, whereby a field is infinite and connects all the objects in it much like electromagnetic fields influence atomic and molecular charged objects or gravity fields influence inanimate objects with mass such as planets and stars. We use field theory to build what we call the Network Field Model. In this model, human actors are modeled as point-like human objects in the field, but this does not exclude robots and other AI entities. However, we will use human actors for ease of explanation.

Influence *between* and investments *in* these point-like human objects are explained as energy exchanges (potential and kinetic) which can be described in terms of three different types of *capital*: financial (assets), human capital (the individual) and social (two or more humans in a network). We explain how energy is both exchanged into different forms, all the while accepting the premise that energy is conserved.

This model is predicated on a field theoretical understanding about the world we live in. We use historical and everyday examples of human activity and describe them in terms of the model. As we do this, we will persistently challenge the reader's understanding of time, position and what it means to be part of an infinite field.

Let us begin.

In our everyday experiences, we often say we "connect" with others in our networks when in actuality, we communicate. We communicate by many seen and unseen means. A network is a model to show that communication. The network depicts lines and dots (representing human objects) and can take on different configurations (and which became the basis for centrality measures in social network analysis in twentieth century research). That communication network presupposes that human objects only become linked together through the process of communicating with each other. Therefore, communication is an ongoing process leading up to organizing, which is the basis of systems theory. It is that assumption—that we are "connected" through the act of communication and that communication leads to organizing—that we challenge. We counter this paradigm by saying that we are *already* influenced by all the objects in the field.

Let us look at some examples:

- How do cells influence each other? We know cells send and receive instructions in two ways. One way is through large molecules such as DNA and messenger

RNA. The other way is even tinier and more invisible to our eyes, using electromagnetic fields. When the electromagnetic pattern is altered, the biological organism, say for example a flatworm, becomes freakishly reconfigured (see TED talk: Electrical blueprints that orchestrate life | Michael Levin, March 31, 2021). Surprisingly, the DNA remains unaltered. So, it would appear that the true code is not the DNA per se, but the electromagnetic sequencing variations in the field.

- Einstein was startled by the experimental results which demonstrated that electronic spins of two electrons separated by a great distance and going at the speed of light in different directions stay instantaneously and perfectly aligned. How could this happen as communication at a speed greater than the speed of light is not possible! He famously quipped that this phenomenon was "spooky at a distance".

Two hundred years ago, alchemists and physicists explained this eerie "connection" as the result of aether, a medium that allowed the propagation of light or communication between objects. But what if "objects" are already influenced by a field requiring no medium for propagation? What if we are already influenced precisely because we are part of a field such as an electromagnetic, gravitational or network field?

The driving force for distinguishing influence from communication was never made more apparent than when twenty-first century companies like AirBnB, Uber, AliBaba and Google conflated the two terms. They made "influence" the new gold standard. These companies built their empires on brokering value-making "clicks" at volume. The centuries-old correlation between labor and return on investment was converted into *the commoditization of influencing*. In the twenty-first century, the act of "connecting" became an act of consumption as a result of influence in the field.

Organizing was never about connecting. Ever. Connection is an illusion, because we are already in the infinite field subjected to influences. Rather, organizing is all about the process of exchanging energy which is not based on either distance or propinquity.

So there are major differences between using twentieth century systems theory, where organizing is the continuous process of communication, and field theory where organizing is the continuous process of influence. The first difference is that communication needs a medium to exchange information whereas influence does not need a medium for the exchange of energy. The second difference is that communication is time dependent. Systems theory is based on processes as they occur in time. Whereas, in the Network Field Model, objects are in the field, influenced instantaneously by the field.

Both theories use an exchange model. Systems theory uses the exchange of information in time using a medium; field theory uses the exchange of energy using a construct, an intermediate particle which we call the Socion for the Network Field Model (comparable to the photon for the electromagnetic field and the graviton for the gravity field), to describe the form of energy exchanged instantaneously and without any medium.

So let us expand this.

We live in a macroscopic world. In this world there are countless tiny microscopic particles that obey the laws of physics. Just because humans are bigger than your average particle does not mean they are not subjected to these same laws. Even with limited knowledge of these laws, our primitive understanding has propelled us to the moon, cured diseases and permitted us to peek into promising interstellar and cellular adventures. Reductionist explanatory metaphors linking behavior with Newtonian physics billiard balls have failed because human behavior is both influenced and curtailed by the network field we are embedded in.

Therefore, we propose a model where energy (in the form of financial, human and social capital) is exchanged between objects in a way that conforms to energy conservation. We use field theory (in lieu of systems theory) to model these energy exchanges. We describe the network field using only limited mathematics, incorporating familiar examples to illustrate the concepts. There is an appendix for those wishing to delve more into the actual mathematics of the model.

The purpose of this book is to introduce the Network Field Model. Volume two discusses the application of the model and volume three uses the model to showcase real world data. Hopefully, our approach, a trifecta of theory, application and use cases, will provide insight and inform innovative solutions for many acute and chronic organizational and societal challenges.

We begin in Section 2 by discussing paradigms currently in use when "organizing". Specifically, we focus on the application of systems theory (a popular twentieth century paradigm) and how it is applied to organizational processes and team dynamics. We demonstrate that while systems theory may provide short-term solutions, it falls short of understanding how working networks actually function and why they, at times, may even disrupt a solution. Human networks are the bedrock of collaborative activity and evolve under the press of technological connection and geographical dispersion.

Section 3 describes the new paradigm: the Network Field Model. In a field there is an exchange of energy, (or "capital", see glossary), between the objects in the field. This exchange can take place in different forms depending on the type of capital involved. In traditional field theory, two types of energy are distinguished: kinetic and potential energy. In the network field model, kinetic energy is associated with financial capital and potential energy is associated with human and social capital. Using these definitions as our ground zero, we can then describe the exchange of capital between objects in a network.

Capital	**Energy**
Human and social capital	Potential energy
Financial capital	Kinetic energy

We also introduce a conceptual diagram that lays out the Network Field Model. We describe each quadrant in successive sections from Sections 4-7 (**Figure 1**).

We begin in Section 4 by describing *learning*. Learning (in the lower left quadrant) is the exchange of potential energy of one human into the potential energy of another human. What do we mean by this? The amount of actual learning is dependent not just on the individual, but on the appreciation of the potential energy of other objects in the network and the trust they place in each other. Here trust is identified in the model as a "weight factor" for the exchange of capital between the objects in the field.

Section 5 describes working (in the lower right quadrant) as the exchange of energy between the potential energy of one actor and the financial capital of another actor. From a financial capital perspective, managers want to optimize a return on their investment. From a potential energy perspective, employees want to optimize the social capital of their employment or their community.

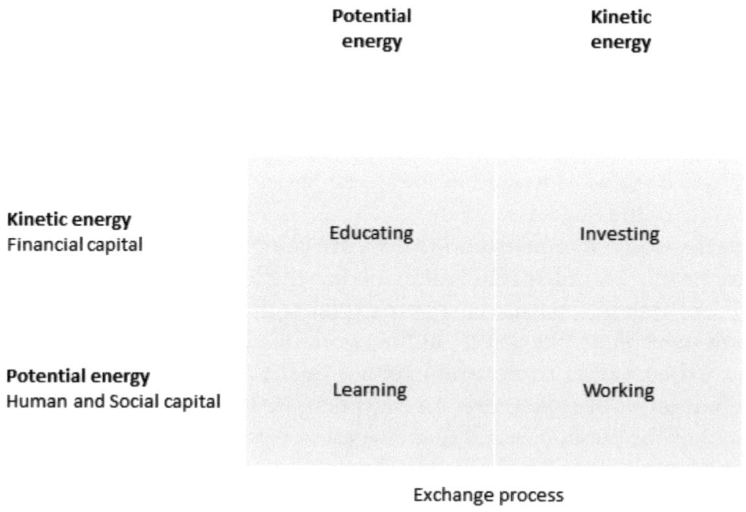

Figure 1.
The Network Field Model.

Section 6 describes *investing* (in the upper right quadrant) as the exchange of financial capital. Here we remind the reader that human and social capital components of our model are position dependent, whereas financial capital is only time dependent. As investments consume time, a return on investment is then measurable and calculable. And, as with any investment, there are risks involved. So, in this section we show the relationship between three components: (1) investing, (2) return on investment, and (3) risk assessment where we use a gap analysis. For example, a "gap" might consist of inadequate or altogether missing connections (social relations) with clients in the context of using a new product or service. This gap can be remediated by understanding the properties required to fill in the gap with the introduction of appropriately matched human capital or social capital. This sounds easy, but it is, in fact, quite sophisticated using the elegant analysis provided by field theory.

Section 7 describes *educating* (in the upper left quadrant) as the act of exchanging financial capital into potential energy. Educating is a classical legacy system. It is centuries old and is centrally organized. With the introduction of new technology and a better understanding of how people actually learn, educational systems have incrementally improved in order to stay abreast of technological advancements. However, the sheer weight of its legacy adds frictional drag prohibiting rapid adaptation in the face of technological disruption. Facing increasing demands for personalized learning and reliable measures for skills and talents, educational systems are in a struggle for relevance.

Section 8 describes how the field model can be put into practice. It is quite commonplace when organizations develop a new strategy, that managers and leaders have difficulty estimating the impact of the new strategy on their employees. Employees are expected to "go along to get along". Naturally, when a new strategy is introduced, people with new knowledge, skills and behaviors will be needed to fill any gaps. Therefore, two strategic investments emerge: (1) investments in the development of existing personnel so they can learn, grow and adapt, and (2) investments in finding and matching new hires with the new jobs generated by the new strategy. We explain why these gaps inevitably arise and their implications for both hierarchical, centralized organizations and networked, decentralized team-based organizations. We provide suggestions for remediation.

Section 9 summarizes our journey. We review the inadequacies of legacy systems for modeling the act of organizing. We argue that organizing can be better explained in terms of a field. Sections 2 and 3 provide the conceptual framework for field theory and then Sections 4–7 describe the different quadrants of the Network Field Model. Our field model is based on a rigorous mathematical description which has been proven in physics and is addressed in the appendix.

Special Note to the Reader:

We want the reader to understand that we are using energy in the way it is used in physics, not the more familiar Newtonian model which deploys concepts like "mass" and "force". In our model, we use energy to explain different types of "capital". We consider humans to be point-like objects in a network in "the field" and their qualities or properties are the result of *investments* in either financial or human and social capital. These different forms of capital explain why energy is transferred between humans.

At the end of the book, you will find suggested readings. We limit our references within the text as it interrupts the logical flow and may be disruptive to the reader.

2. The problem of organizing

It seems
as if we all
do the same
with the
same input
but somehow
the results
are different.

All our life
we try
to manage each
process
being standard
as a goal
instead of
understanding that
together
we get results
being not
the same.

The human act of "organizing" has evolved over-time [1]. The earliest records of primordial hunter-gatherers show that kinship and trade networks were inevitably subsumed by a nobility class arising from increased agrarian output. Wheels and the physics of water created the great pyramids but it took over 6 millenia to fashion the smelting of iron and the production of steel into large-scale "machines" leveraging the work of just a few men to several thousand. This nascent technological innovation gave way to industrialization and urbanization in the nineteenth and twentieth centuries. As knowledge became increasingly specialized, the "transfer" of this accumulated knowledge evolved from simple apprenticeships to the formation of professions. The professions were merely ways of organizing and credentialing knowledge, an outgrowth of knowledge production centralized in schools, colleges and universities. Now, these massive educational-industrial complexes are undergoing disruption due to digital platforms. As a result, knowledge production and learning are becoming increasingly fragmented and decentralized.

One outgrowth of industrialization was conceptualizing the world as a system, whereby knowledge was encoded in the machine and humans were tethered to the machines for their management and upkeep. A prerequisite for managing the duality of the human-machine enterprise was the concept of financial capital supported by the people who had the knowledge and skills to optimize and sustain the system. When problems arose, the organizing premise was that any problem was innate to that particular domain of knowledge. This meant that economists described the economic system, psychologists described the human mind, sociologists described small groups and organizations and anthropologists described human cultures and so on. Within each professional domain, problems were circumscribed into a "system" composed of three parts: (1) inputs from the environment, (2) internal processes and (3) outputs to the environment. The system was managed by feedback loops and managerial steering actions. Using this approach, the mechanical (the factory) and the intellectual (the logical processes) could be optimized.

So, modeling knowledge was predicated on the disciplines which in turn were organized into professions, silo-esque structures designed for knowledge storage. Every discipline and its derived associated professions dispensed solutions for many specialized problems (see Foucault [2]).

But there's a catch.

Problem sets were predicated on the assumption that the system was bounded, sustained and reinforced by its associated profession. This is a classic (and ironic) feedback loop in that the solutions were governed by how the problem was defined. The resulting set of specialized "solutions" might indeed work for a limited period, but they had no internal coherence across problem sets because "reality" was apportioned and assigned to its appropriate discipline. "Systems thinking" was the accumulation, not the amalgamation, of subsystems. Therefore, systems theory was systematic but not systemic. It was constrained and sustained by professional blinders. Here are just two examples.

1. When Einstein was working on quantum physics he was not innovating; he was simply trying to explain why particles behaved the way they did because it represented a problem in the current theory at the time. The group of physicists including de Broglie, Heisenberg, Planck, Ehrenfeld, Lorenz and Bohr discovered that the scientific model of reality was not fully correct. The real innovations came later when scientists started to apply the field model of reality to existing processes.

2. In manufacturing, reducing error and demonstrating ROI (Return on Investment) has built up our economies and increased the GDP (Gross Domestic Product) of many countries. This type of process orientation is correct only from the perspective of financial capital; investments in highly efficient processes deliver a high return. The return is even higher the more improved those processes become until they can be standardized and accomplished by machines. The return on the financial capital is then recycled by investors in a continuous flow of making more financial capital by using only financial capital. It's a classic feedback loop.

To summarize, systems theory orients our worldview to "process" information and "process" problems to improve effectiveness and efficiency. We produce a product, service or knowledge, we detect any corresponding problems in manufacturing, processing or research respectively. We then step outside the flow of work, solve those problems and then step back into production. Wash, rinse, repeat. The improvement is based on the classic feedback loop. We did not *prevent* problems, we only solved them as they arose. We have been essentially *reactive* which brings us to an uncomfortable realization.

If economic activity is based on financial or knowledge capital, then raising your children or helping your grandmother is not. Only when the parent hires a service and pays a professional fee is the activity deemed economic activity. Otherwise, as valuable an activity as raising children or helping extended family may be, it is not classified as economic activity. This paradigm has had a very negative effect on a wide range of social activities simply because social activities are not interpreted as economic activities. As such, there is no return on investment when the activity is not valued.

All of human activity is occurring every day in what could be imagined as the network field of human organization - in families, communities, education and businesses (see Levi-Strauss [3]). To address the forgotten activities that we just described, we use a model that is based on field theory [4].

A field can be described mathematically by a formula, a Lagrangian, which gives us a value for the energy in the field at each point in space and time. In the case of a scalar field, this value is numeric. For example, the temperature field over the earth is a scalar field. At each point in space and time, we can measure the temperature and will find a numeric value.

Energy is described as kinetic energy and potential energy and the Lagrangian, L, of the field at a certain point in space and time as the difference between the kinetic and the potential energy. We adopt the use of this field theory because as the reader will see, it accounts for all these forgotten activities as well as other classical economic activities.

Our model is based on a scalar network field and defines capital as energy. In this model, the kinetic energy is the financial capital (the appreciation of the assets owned by the object) and the potential energy is the combination of human (knowledge, skills and autonomy of the object) and social capital (the relations with other objects) in the network. This "field" conceptualization is wholly apart from the traditional systems theory paradigm as systems theory could never conceive of exchanges between human objects as energy within a field.

Capital	Energy
Human and social capital	Potential energy
Financial capital	Kinetic energy

We use our field model to describe what happens when an object moves in the field at a certain moment in time. The "capital" (e.g. energy) of that human object changes when it is influenced by other objects in the field. This may sound abstract, but it is the foundation for a classification scheme of activities. We define four different types of exchange or activities:

- *Learning:* exchanging your own potential energy into someone else's potential energy
- *Working*: exchanging your own potential energy, that is, human and social capital, into kinetic energy, financial capital
- *Investing:* exchanging your own kinetic energy into someone else's kinetic energy
- *Educating:* exchanging your own kinetic energy into potential energy

These activities are embedded in the conceptual diagram in **Figure 1** (presented below as a convenience to the reader). This conceptual diagram logically organizes what happens when energy or capital is exchanged in a field.

This model shifts activities away from centralized hierarchical systems to decentralized connections in the network field. For example,

> *... consider the 21st century transformation from centralized processing to decentralized collaboration in the fashion industry. Previously, companies looked for ways to minimize stock, minimize financial capital in assets, and increase turnover time by anticipating style and outsourcing production of those styles using cheap labor in developing countries.*

> *When this centralized processing is decentralized, designers can collaborate in networks with possible buyers thereby anticipating what people want. Based on novel designs, a person will order a dress (for example) which will then be produced as a unique dress for that person. This can be done at low cost because automation produces the pattern for the cutting machines and other machines stitch the dress together.*

The fact that technology platforms have created a tipping point for industrial transformation only further demonstrates how digitization decentralizes the way people connect and work. Centralized control and ownership produce solutions that still trump decentralized alternatives at the moment, but how long this will continue remains unclear.

The democratization and fragmentation of information are neither utopian or dystopian. It represents a profound paradigmatic shift from centralized hierarchical systems to decentralized connections. We may all be created equally, but we are not connected equally. However, one fact remains: we are *all* connected. And it is the recognition of this ubiquitous connection that moves us away from egotistically being at the center of our silo-ed or tribal cabals to recognizing our position in a field and part of an infinite universe.

3. Field theory

Accepting that
we all are
a part
of a whole
teaches us
what we
are
and who we
need to
learn from and
give
to fulfill
a goal
together.

In the previous section we discussed systems theory and its limitations and introduced a new conceptual model, the Network Field Model, based in field theory. In this section, we delve further into field theory before launching into successive sections describing how the Network Field Model explains different types of organizing.

In our introduction, we described different examples of how a field houses energy exchanges for people, cells and electronic spins. The idea of a "field" has been a riddle wrapped in a mystery inside an enigma. Physicists and social scientists alike have debated this concept of a field:

- Physicists have long struggled with the concept of a field since the nineteenth century. Early thought identified aether (also known as ether) as a transmission medium, a space-filling substance or *field*, that existed for the propagation of electromagnetic or gravitational forces in much the same way as sound is transmitted in the air. Gravitational waves and then quantum theory overtook aether as a working model and then the idea of a field became firmly established in science (see [5]).

- The French sociologist Bourdieu (building on the work of Marcel Mauss [6]) introduced a field-like concept, called "habitus" to describe how humans exchanged gifts or goods and how these acts of exchange over time affected the larger societal structure of relationships [7]. Bourdieu was describing gift exchange, not energy exchange, per se, but he was closely approximating the idea of a field, including concepts of time and position dependency.

Our conceptual approach builds on both these approaches from the natural and social sciences: (1) the use of field theory to describe the properties of the objects, and (2) the exchange of energy between the objects in the field.

3.1 The field

In the Network Field Model (NFM) we describe a field and its influence on (human) objects in that field. In this description, we state that there is **one** infinite field and that the field influences objects without any intermediate substance such as aether. This means that all human objects have one amount of kinetic energy and one amount of potential energy and all influence each other through the field.

To describe the field, we suggest using a scalar field, so the field has a real value at each point in four-dimensional spacetime. The field is event-driven. An event is described by (1) the field, (2) the function of the energy distribution, (3) the properties of the objects in the field and (4) their relative distance from each other.

Grounding principles:

1. A field follows the principles of nature: energy is conserved and entropy increases.

2. A field is composed of kinetic and potential energy.

3. Kinetic energy is time-dependent.

4. Potential energy is relative position-dependent.

A *network* in the field is a subset of human objects who have a common goal to be fulfilled. As such, a network is a *social construct* because the set of human objects that make up the network have decided upon a common goal and work together to achieve that goal. Therefore, a human object can be a member of multiple networks simultaneously, for example, working on multiple teams in the same organization or the community.

What does it mean for a human object to *move* in a network field? This is called an event and each event influences the energy of an individual human object, while the total energy stays the same, that is, energy is conserved.

To illustrate an event, we use the notions of **time dependent** in our field description to mean that certain properties of a human object change in time. We also use **position dependent** to mean that the properties of the human object stay the same over time when no events in the field take place. However, when an event takes place, it then becomes position dependent and when this happens, the properties of the object can change. This means that the relative distance between objects could also change.

For example, in **Figure 2**, we show the two-dimensional position in a network and the time. In the diagram, the position of Alice (A) and Bob (B) is indicated in a small network consisting of five members (A, B, C, D, E) at time 0, t = 0. At time 1, t = 1, the position of Alice (A) and Bob (B) will be changed and this results in a different relative distance between the two. At time 2, t = 2, the relative position is again different.

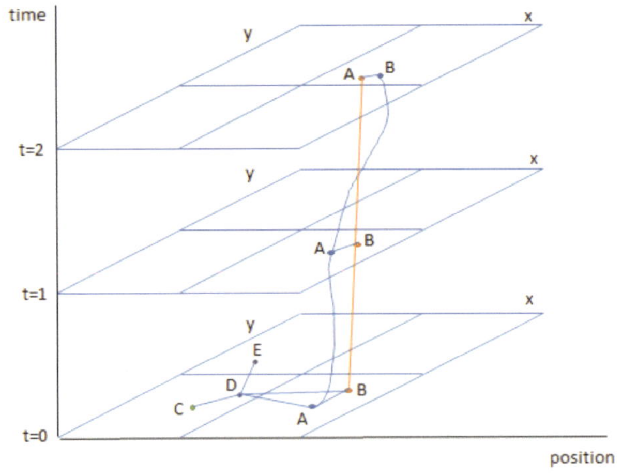

Figure 2.
Changing relative distance in time.

To summarize, the network field describes the possible events between the objects depending on their properties and the relative distance. The relative distance between the objects, r, is defined by the shortest path in the network between the two objects. The objects are in the field and the density of the field is defined by the total number of links, which are measured as symmetric and asymmetric links in the network. The density is given by the total number of links between all objects in the network, but in our model, we only consider the total number of links between two objects since we use this to determine the trust (as defined in the glossary) between those actors.

All human objects in the field influence each other. As in the aforementioned, any subset of human objects can become a network when they share a common goal or interest. To describe this influence, we use a different coordinate system (see **Figure 3**) based on the relative distance as defined by the path distance in a network (direct or indirect relation to the other human object) and the azimuthal angles.

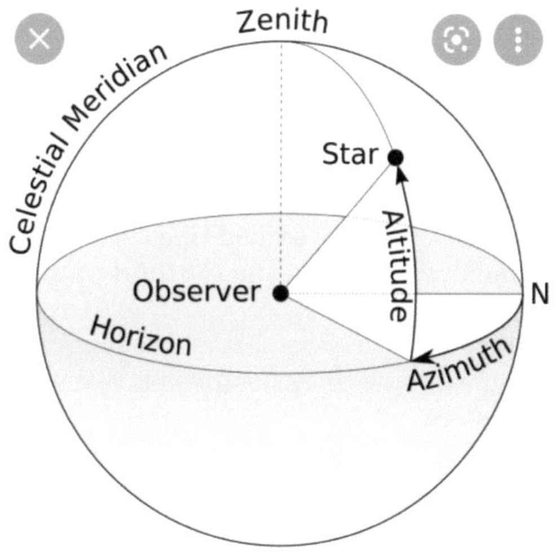

Figure 3.
An illustration of the azimuth angle.

The first step in describing this network is to understand the relative position of each object. Therefore, we choose one object as the center of the coordinate system (t,0,0,0) and position all other objects in the network (which is a closed system) at a relative distance of r. So, the network representation in the coördinate system is based on t, the time, r, the relative distance between two nodes and the two azimuthal angles, θ, ζ. Since this is symmetric around the azimuthal angles (an azimuth is an angular measurement in a spherical coordinate system), we can rotate the network around the centre of the coordinate system and in doing so, we have essentially constructed a sphere with all the objects inside the sphere.

3.2 The exchange of energy between objects in a field

Describing objects as point-like objects in the network field allows us to determine the total energy and as such the total capital. Each object, has a certain amount of energy or capital available. The total capital is composed of three kinds of capital, financial, human and social capital.

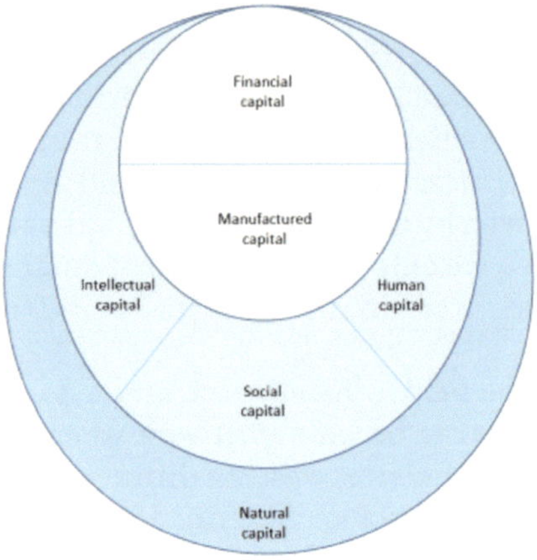

Figure 4.
IIF model of capital.

These concepts have a long half-life, dating back to Adam Smith and as recently as the International Institute of Finance (IIF). By way of example, we will use the IIF conceptual model (as shown in **Figure 4**) to compare how our model both embraces and departs from these concepts. In the IIF model we see in the center a combination of manufactured and financial capital, a second ring consisting of human capital, sociological capital and intellectual capital and the third ring, the natural capital.

- In our model, we merge the IIF financial and manufactured capital to become financial capital. The reason for this adjustment is that we define financial capital as the sum of all the assets.

- We also combine the IIF partitions of human capital with intellectual capital. In our case, human capital is defined by the value of the knowledge, skills and autonomy of an object.

- We have social capital defined as the value of the relations between the objects in the network. So in our description we assume that each object has its own individual properties but also has a relation with the other objects.

Our model is based on the science of fields. In any field, there are two kinds of energy: potential and kinetic energy. Potential energy is dependent on an actor's position in the field and it can be transformed into kinetic energy. For example, according to Newton, a ball is resting in your hand as you stand on the top of a tower. The ball has potential energy because of the gravity field and will be changed into kinetic energy when you release the ball. The movement or acceleration is the increase in kinetic energy and is related to the field at a certain point in time.

We state that the human capital and social capital in the IIF model are *combined* in our Network Field Model and this represents the *potential energy* of an object in the network field at a point in time. The value of the capital is dependent on the position of the object in the network. What is important to realize is that the human and social capital may stay the same, but that the *value* might change as a result of exchange (influence) with other objects in the field.

DOI: http://dx.doi.org/10.5772/intechopen.100574

The financial capital is kinetic energy. In our model the kinetic energy is independent of the position of the object in the field since the value of the assets belonging to an object is valued in a global market instead of only in the network. It is dependent on time because the appreciation of those assets in a global market fluctuates over time.

Capital	Energy
Human and social capital	Potential energy
Financial capital	Kinetic energy

Now we can see that the potential energy and kinetic energy are interchangeable. Potential energy, for example, human and social capital, can be changed into financial capital by using both to make money. On the other hand, kinetic energy, for example, financial capital, can be changed into human or social capital by paid training or by financial investments in social relations.

These energy exchanges take place in the field, in general, and in networks, in particular. As we described earlier, a network is a social construct, a subset of human objects in the field that have a shared goal they are trying to achieve. Hierarchies and heterarchies (networked hierarchies) are also social constructs that describe organizational strategies on a larger scale and encompass many networks. Although we tend to think of these hierarchical and heterarchical structures as fixed, they are porous structures permeated by the networks in the field. This fluidity is an outcome of being in the field and can sometimes result in unintended consequences such as accidental innovation, simultaneous discoveries and fraud.

3.3 Optimizing exchange: the special case of flow

In systems theory, the interaction "duality" of action-reaction brings people into a working production state. But the real challenge for any working group is to *synchronously* coordinate activities to achieve the optimum state of "flow". Flow is a special case in the field where all objects in the group act as one. Mihaly Csikszentmihalyi, the author of flow, described its characteristics but he could never measure it mathematically [8]. However, the Network Field Model makes it entirely possible to measure flow as an energy exchange for production states such as team sports, working activities and learning. We discuss flow further in the next section on learning.

4. Learning

Placing trust
in someone
is not
depending on
relative positions
in a society
or on the
field in which
we all exist.

It is not even
dependent
on time
but develops
by learning
each other
changing our
way of under
standing
resulting in a
very special love.

In the next four sections, we describe the impact of the model on the exchange of capital in four different areas. The first area is learning, the exchanging of the potential energy of one object to the potential energy of another object. The next area is working or exchanging the potential energy of one object to the kinetic energy of another object. The third area is investing, or the exchange of the kinetic energy of one object to the kinetic energy of another object. The fourth is educating, or the exchange of kinetic energy of one object to the potential energy of another object (**Figure** 5).

The first step in learning is usually socialization where people are working together on the same problem and exchanging their tacit knowledge in the process. What is tacit knowledge [9]?

> *Let us consider the act of learning to ride a bicycle. Most of us learned this activity when we were young. Our parents or older siblings were helping us by lending support and advice when riding and after a few falls, we eventually learned to ride the bike without the training wheels. Once learned, it's difficult to forget, or as the old saying goes, "it's just like riding a bike." Now try and explain bicycling to someone else. How do you ride your bike, how do you put your feet on the pedals, your hands on the handlebars and still manage to move forward all the while maintaining your balance! The explicit explanation comes from physics. When wheels are spinning fast, they want to go in the same direction. In other words, they behave as gyroscopes maintaining the motion of the bike. When you stop, you fall. But the explicit explanation is not what most of us heard as children. The knowledge of how to ride a bike is fundamentally tacit knowledge, or "felt" knowledge. That is, it has to be experientially learned and that is how we are using the word "learning" here in the book.*

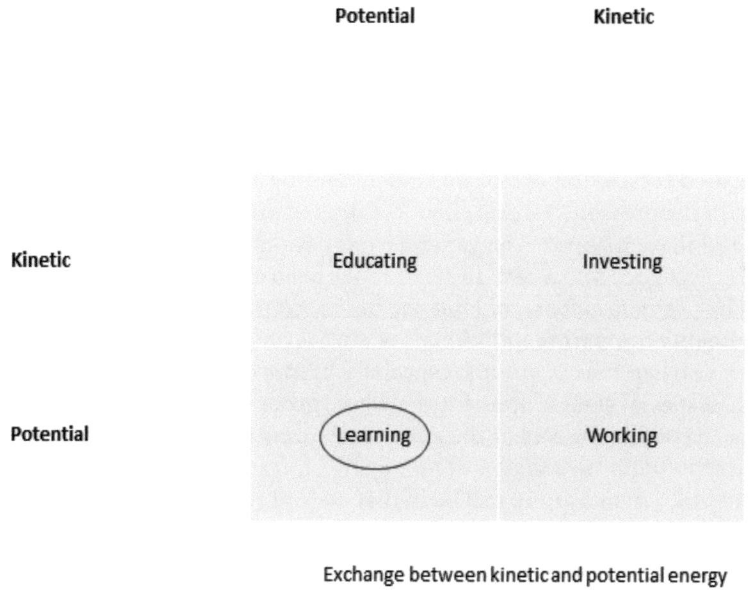

Figure 5.
The Network Field Model—learning.

People in teams for example, either have all the necessary knowledge and skills available or if they do not, they know how to get it. Being part of a working group and solving a problem together brings about a deeper learning experience as opposed to the knowledge presented by a teacher in a classroom. When a problem is solved by a student group, for example, the solution is "sticky" and generally stays in the brain much longer as opposed to the shorter half-life of simple memorization for a final exam. We argue that the major difference between (1) learning by aggregating explicit information (studying for a final exam) and (2) learning by socializing is the presence of trust.

4.1 The case for trust

As we mentioned, socialization is a critical step in the learning process because it leverages the trust in the relations between people for the exchange of potential energy. To be able to learn together, we must trust each other. Therefore trust can be thought of as a **weight factor** for the probability of the exchange of potential energy between different objects in the network. Essentially, trust is an assurance of the character, ability, or authenticity of someone. For that reason, the appreciation of potential energy may be quite high. However, if the trust is low, then the chance of exchange is greatly diminished. By using trust as an adjustable weight factor we can optimize the network to determine the trust needed for a particular situation where a particular goal is to be achieved. Based on that determination, one can "invest in trust" by investing in social capital, for example, the social relations within the network [10].

What is it about trust? We accept data provided by people we trust in a very different way from people we do not trust. Even Adam Smith emphasized how trust is used to lower uncertainty and vulnerability by altering the threshold for information to be accepted. So, let us distinguish between interpersonal trust and task-related trust. Interpersonal trust is necessary for taking in and accepting information while task-related trust is necessary when working in groups. Both types of trust exist in groups when working together. Each member has to trust the other to do the right thing, reach the mutual goal, and at the same time trust each other to exchange information. Therefore, interpersonal trust is the weight factor when *potential energy* is exchanged.

Task-related trust is important for understanding "flow" in a group. As we mentioned in the previous section, flow is a type of optimization that occurs both in the group and in each object. The general explanation of flow is that the brain of an individual object goes into a certain state. It has been described as *though time stood still, everything became automatic, I did not realize what I was doing until I finished.* Those statements come from individuals when they were in a state of flow.

But flow also happens in groups, especially in sports. There are numerous examples of a special state of flow for the whole group in the same moment. After the moment has passed, members of the network express the same experiences of *feeling no time, the other player was always at the right spot, it was as if we were acting as one.* So how is it possible when a group can be in that state at the same time even when there is no or almost no physical interaction between the objects?

When we use the Network Field Model as our starting point, we can describe objects in a network where the exchange of capital is taking place synchronously since potential energy is time-independent. We explain this state of flow as an "optimization in the field" meaning that the needed kinetic and potential energy in the total group does not require the processing of additional external data for the group goal to be fulfilled. Therefore, the optimized state has been achieved **before** group action starts. In the example of a sports team, we know that a leader trusts the members of the team and the team members also trust the leader. All work together to achieve a common goal. Once the action has begun, no exchange is required or necessary as the group is in an optimized state. This is expressed as members seamlessly anticipating the movements of the others. It is entirely possible to calculate the trust between members of a network, or a team, and develop an algorithm to pro-actively produce the desired "flow" effect. We discuss this further in Section 8.

To summarize, we have described learning as a network in a field connecting objects. We consider the appreciation of the available capital of an object in the network by the other objects and the trust shared between them. The *appreciation* determines the value of the kinetic and potential energy, whereas the *trust* acts as a weighting factor for the exchange of potential energy between two objects. The *relative distance* is the shortest path between two objects in the network, and the *density* is the measured amount of (a)synchronous links (contacts) between the objects.

4.2 Machine learning

Can this process of learning be performed by machines? In the 1990s knowledge management (KM) systems were introduced to source existing knowledge in an organization. The KM software engines largely failed.

Author's note: The government requested that I assess how well a knowledge management system might work since approximately 60% of their employees were older than 55 years. The loss of expertise was imminent as they were retiring. The request consisted of asking everyone what knowledge they had and to input it into the KM software system. A problem emerged: the knowledge description in the system was incomplete. In order to better understand this problem, I conducted a small network analysis with employees older than 60 years to ascertain what they knew and with whom they had contact. The results were unexpected. The older professionals were only talking outside the department about what they were doing and why. So socialization was occurring in the informal system, what is sometimes quaintly referred to as "networking". Knowledge management systems were largely a failure because they could never track or mimic informal system environments.

Tacit knowledge is not a characteristic of machine learning. The challenge is to make tacit knowledge from objects explicit through programmed algorithms using observable external data. Therefore, it is entirely possible that machines construct their own algorithms to create knowledge and even more intriguing—autonomy. For that reason, intelligent machines could be integrated with human networks to fulfill certain goals.

In Section 8 we describe the architecture when optimizing a network for a certain goal. This is based on starting with a network and calculating the total capital of each object. The collective goal of the network determines the kinetic energy, the financial part necessary for the investments, and the potential energy, the knowledge, skills and autonomy plus any additional relations needed in the network. It is safe to assume that there will be gaps in fulfilling the goal; so there has to be some learning to bridge the gaps. This can be done by (1) educating other objects from *outside* the network, (2) learning from other trusted objects *within* the network or (3) by adding AI machines to fill the gap.

In conclusion, learning is one of the most difficult activities to be undertaken. It is linked to socialization and involves the exchange of tacit knowledge. Parenting and apprenticeship are the only two recorded ways human tacit knowledge exchange is accomplished. But tacit knowledge involves more than the child copying the behavior of the parents or the student copying the work of the teacher. In both cases, socialization is used to create trust and trust catalyzes the exchange of potential energy.

There are downsides to learning this way. The apprentice acquires knowledge from his or her mentor. Most knowledge has a "sell by" date, and unfortunately in educational systems, old knowledge is perpetuated. Students learn from professors by interning or by apprenticing in the skilled trades. The result is that they are learning knowledge that has a natural shelf life and that the knowledge *value* may have decreased or altogether expired. Even when research shows knowledge has reached its expiration date, it persists in the system. So, while socialization (and trust) provides a familiar (or familial) feel to learning, it can also block innovation and change. Add to this challenge that apprenticeship is expensive because of the time and effort it takes to do it well. Therefore, it cannot be scaled effectively. Unfortunately, humans have found no better way to accomplish learning.

5. Working

Our whole life
as complex
structures
physical objects
we increase entropy.

We create all
the time
more information
but in the
same time
heat up
by eating
the structures
around us
building chaos.

In our model, we have made a distinction between financial capital, the human capital and the social capital. This distinction has an impact on the way we think about work as an economic activity [11]. As presented in the diagram our definition of work is the exchange of potential energy into financial capital (**Figure 6**).

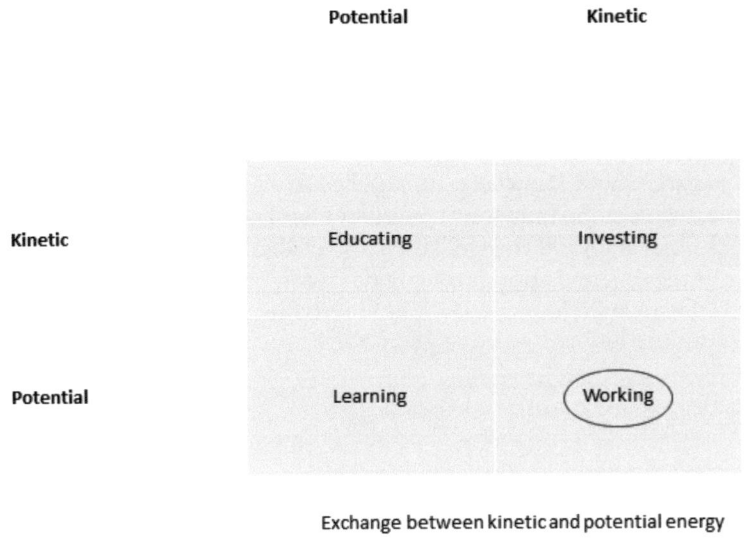

Figure 6.
The Network Field Model—working.

Exchange of financial capital:

1. Work is the exchange of potential energy into kinetic energy or financial capital. For example, when I clean my home in my free time, that work is not considered economic, but when someone else cleans my home and I pay for it, then it is. We will bring this up again later in the section.

2. Let us dig a little deeper. I have knowledge about how to make wooden doors. There are 10 people in my network and 8 of them or 80% need a door. Therefore, my human capital is highly valued; my stock price is high. I am asked to produce doors for two people in the network for 1000 dollars per door. I do this. Therefore, I have exchanged my human capital for financial capital. As a result, my human capital decreases because now only 6 of the initial 8 people (or 60%) need or want a door. As my human capital is exchanged into financial capital, my human capital decreases and my financial capital increases. The increase in my financial capital is a direct result of people in my network investing or trading their financial capital for a door. When all the remaining 6 doorless people in my network request a door and pay me for the doors, then the appreciation of my capabilities drops to almost zero (there might always be someone who wants a door in the future). This is the supply-demand model.

3. The exchange of financial capital can also be brokered by third parties. When a teacher offers knowledge to students at a government or public school, the students are not paying the teacher. The government is paying the teacher, so the production value of the teacher is measured by the government subsidy as well as the parents of the student who pay government taxes. The same logic applies to doctors in a hospital. The simplest way of illustrating this is that the doctor is paid by the insurance company and the patient pays the insurance company.

In the description of financial capital in section three we stated that financial capital is dependent on time, whereas human and social capital are dependent on the (relative) position in the network. Return on investment (ROI) describes the change in financial capital over time. We remind the reader that we have postulated that financial capital is used inside the closed system of the network. Therefore, it has to follow the law of total energy conservation. So, return on investment simply means that when I employ others to use their capabilities, then my financial capital increases and I get a return. This process of exchanging financial capital by paying for production is primordial and started when society evolved from tribes into clans into kingdoms.

- In a tribe, we lived in a closed system and your capabilities were important for the tribe and were valued. There was no payment.

- When trade was introduced, tribes exchanged their assets with each other. Rules were created to govern valuation, creating some competition and along with that, defense systems to protect the assets.

- Kingdoms needed armies, so soldiers were conscripted. Kingdoms also needed specialized people for managing these assets, so bureaucracies were constructed to provide administration, policy and laws.

- The Industrial Revolution was the logical evolution of society converting human capital into financial capital with the help of machines. Ownership becomes an important property of human capital. We assume for our purposes that the total capital of an object is such that the object owns his or her capital, that is, they are not slaves or indentured servants. Therefore, when an object has capital that can be used for the production of certain products or services, that capital is valued and owned by that object, not by the employer. The employer owns what is produced. Two cases illustrate:

a When the object has his own company, that object is exchanging his own human capital, his knowledge, skills and autonomy into financial capital and the value of that product is part of his own assets. He can then trade that product in the market.

b. On the other hand, when the object is an employee, there is a contract between the employer and employee that whatever is produced using human and social capital is owned by the employer. The employer is paying a salary for using that capital. So a "job" is defined as using available capabilities in a specific environment to produce something paid for by an employer. According to most international laws the human and social capital will always be owned by the object even while he or she is an employee. This is what we have been practicing up until very recently. We are using financial capital as the basic ingredient for economic activities in society.

It is important to keep this in mind when we discuss the position of intelligent machines. Machines also produce knowledge using their knowledge and skills, but have no ownership and, in this sense, are similar to slaves. Everything is owned by the person who used his or her financial capital to procure or buy the intelligent machine.

In our model we assume that the total energy, for example, capital, in a closed network is conserved. This means that when an object has capabilities that are highly appreciated by other objects in the network, the other objects will start to learn from that object. So, what happens when a professor offers his lecture notes on social media for free? What happens when we make open-source software? What happens when doctors do not ask money for their service, but receive food and shelter instead? Are we in a devolution?

No.

In this case, we are evolving from a financial capital society to a social capital society. Now let us return to the example of cleaning the home. When I clean my home by myself, I generate no economic value, but as soon as I pay someone to do it for me, it is economic value. Let us consider an alternative path. When I do not pay the person that cleans my home but instead trade their service for another such as repairing a computer or building a door without financial compensation, then we are back to no economic valuation again but with one important difference. We have traded services *and created social capital*.

So, our point is this: By trying to translate everything into economic value, we create a society where we are using the wrong measurements to determine what is fit for purpose.

For example, what happens when a professor's knowledge is externalized in a book and then the book is published as open-source? As soon as it has been published, the professor is not needed anymore to transfer the knowledge; it is available for free for everyone. We are creating a zero-cost economy. Zero cost economy means we offer a service and it costs nothing extra when there are more users of the service. Once the investment is done, there are no more extra costs even when there are more users of the service. Of course, this is not the end of the story.

In the decade between 2010 and 2020, many companies came to market with this model. Normally they charge a fee per unit of time to earn money. This means they are dependent on their market penetration, that is, the amount of connections they have with customers. In the case of Google, their model is to offer the service, a search engine, for free and then earn revenue through advertising. On the other hand, some platforms offer their service in this zero-cost model for free or on voluntary donations, like Wikipedia. Applying this model to the products of a professor (without publishers as commercial intermediates) offers a better use of human capital without extra costs. So instead of a student buying expensive books for a certain course, the information is readily available for free through an online distribution platform, downloadable by millions of people without extra costs. For example, the book you are reading now, our book is an example of this model as it is published on open source.

When we have a society based on social capital instead of financial capital there will be some residual challenges. One challenge is that we still need financial capital to live and to pay for our daily needs. Assume all the food everybody needs, all education and public transport, all communication and healthcare are free. "Free" means in this case that the financial capital needed is paid for by taxes (mostly value-added taxes so more consumption means more taxes). This means that we do not have jobs in those areas. People can bid or subscribe to win projects. This could be a paid project or a non-paid project.

In a social capital-based society there could be a split between what is *needed* to live on a day-to-day basis and what is *wanted* as extra. This is a split between a basic income and the extra luxury which has to be earned separately. The idea is that a basic income for everyone is earned by the total GDP, which in the future is mostly earned by machines with artificial intelligence, and the sales taxes, where the extra luxury is earned by everyone.

In a society based on economic principles, a financial capital society, all the production data must be owned by the central management of the capital. In a social capital society, the data still have to be available but are owned by the objects. To summarize, we see evolution in three broad stages. (1) Originally, the human capital of the people in the tribe was used and no data or a minimal amount of data was used to manage the production. (2) The next stage is a financial capital society where the installed management uses all the data available for economic, defense, health, education and other reasons. (3) The third stage is a social capital society where both actors, the organizations and the individuals, use the data but where the data is owned and maintained by the individual objects.

We are transitioning to the third stage now. The power of the owners of vast networks (social media and technology platforms) is necessary to sustain the connections between people. These owners act as economic powers owning the data and using the data to increase their return on investment. So, in fact they are using the capital in the network to increase their capital without asking permission for it. Abuse and censorship can result. This is mitigated by new laws like the GDPR, the international ruling on privacy protection. Additionally, legal concerns about the misuse of data can sometimes push the owners of these networks to adjust their strategy. Regardless, this market gap is bridged by the implementation of separate "wallets" owned by individuals.

5.1 Bridging and Innovation

In our model, we have defined a closed system with a fixed amount of capital. The only way investment can be made into the total capital of the network is to come from outside of the network through bridging to other networks. Bridging is the act of connecting to other networks. This is how energy from outside the closed system comes into the closed system. The bridges are formed by a connection between two actors in two different networks, which allow for the exchange of capital. This could be the network of venture capitalists offering financial capital to new ventures or new networks of actors, or consultancy firms offering knowledge and experience from other cases. As long as there are bridges to other networks and the bridges are used to exchange capital between the two networks, invention and innovation will lead to the creation of new capital in the system [12].

5.2 Applying the model for working

Now we apply the model to discuss work, the exchange of potential, human and social, capital into kinetic, financial, capital. We see that objects are offering their (potential) capital to employers to earn money, to get financial capital in exchange. They need that financial capital to be able to buy the goods they want or need. This assumes the economic definition of work, exchanging potential energy for financial capital and does not take into account the non-economic work like supporting your grandparents, supporting the neighborhood or other volunteer activities.

The application of the model can be used in two circumstances. The first is in the recruitment or match-making process where a job is matched to the capabilities of the applicant. The second addresses the larger strategic process of an organization, where a shift in strategy leads to a reorientation of the goals of the organization.

5.2.1 Recruitment match-up

Currently, recruitment processes are rather inefficient. Management agrees on a new position and informs the human resources department. The description is published on a platform which could result in thousands of applications. All these applications must be processed and information verified. After a selection of recruits has been made, interviews have to be planned and the final selection process is started. This whole process is conservatively estimated to cost about € 10.000 per position. Add to this cost, the fact that a new recruit is not effective immediately. A job description only lists the functional competencies but does not take into consideration every social aspect of the job. Job interviews are usually wholly insufficient (inversely related to outcome in some research studies!) to determine how a new recruit might operate in a team. The unintended consequence is that many new recruits fail because they are not the right fit. This Type I statistical error is costly, producing high attrition rates for companies.

There are several reasons for this expensive, cumbersome and ineffective process. The first reason revolves around determining the job description in the organization. A job description is based on functional requirements which have their roots in the Industrial Revolution, when humans worked in concert with and alongside machines. For this reason, the European Union has instituted the European Qualification Framework (EQF). In this framework, existing knowledge, skills and autonomy of an object are taken into account as well as the job role and the qualification or quantity of education needed to perform that job.

The second reason is more Post-Industrial and revolves around the use of digital platforms for recruitment. The business model of these platforms is based on collecting applicant information and building a database. These platforms, however, are not auditors and cannot determine the fidelity of applicant information. The result is that applicants can produce statements that under- or over-represent their skills or completely miscategorize them. For example, statements like "I studied management at Harvard" may refer to a one-month online course.

The third reason is a very common problem involving implicit bias, most of which is predicated on the racial, ethnic or national background and gender. One way to avoid implicit bias is to have an algorithm that sorts the properties. However, implicit bias creeps into the interview process and is one of the more difficult problems to overcome.

We propose a different approach where the match-up is based on two-way digital conversations that qualify an applicant before the biased interview process begins. We discuss this in Section 8. This approach does not eliminate bias, it only diminishes the possibility of bias derailing the match-up process.

5.2.2 Strategic match-up

When management determines a new direction or new business development for the organization, this creates a dynamic tension where hierarchy meets networking. What do we mean? The hierarchical structure of any organization is a competency-based system, cataloged within the HR database. However, the social capital, rooted in the organizational network, is virtually invisible simply because it has not been measured.

So what happens when organizations try to find the right people to achieve their new business strategy?

What many organizations typically do is fall back on the hierarchy: that is, determine which competencies are required, who has to be fired and what new people have to be hired. Most organizations achieve these goals in a ham-fisted way. As a result, many valuable employees are made redundant when in fact they have valuable but "unknown" qualifications (unknown because they are not measured). In other words, they *could* have been an asset. This is what we call the Type II statistical error. The most famous example of a Type II statistical error is the story of Bill Gates, who as a young employee at IBM was not recognized for his qualifications and left the organization. He started Microsoft and the rest is history. What might have happened had he been recognized for his competences and stayed?? Who knows? He simply got away. Normally, heads of organizations or HR departments think that they can recognize their talented internal people, but they really cannot do this unless they have a more objective system in place.

In Section 8, we show how our model anticipates and optimizes the match-up between the undertaking of a new strategic direction of the organization and the effect it has on the strategic direction of the different teams and networks within the organization. This can be done in 3 steps: (1) management determines the qualifications needed to fulfill the new strategic goal, (2) an algorithm matches these qualifications to existing competencies of the employee pool, (3) this results in a "probability score" for each team to fulfill the said goal. When the probability is too low, a decision can be made to recruit from outside or change the goal.

In conclusion, this approach is superior because leaders can better determine who is part of what team (internal matching), who is leftover, (reassignment), who should leave the organization (made redundant), and which roles should be filled by new employees (recruitment).

6. Investing

They told me
that money
is necessary and
should be
used to
make more.

But somehow
it became
clear to me
that happiness
is not only made
by money
but also by
the impact
made on others
the increase in
the total
capital together
making me
richer.

In the previous sections, we have explained learning and working as examples of converting different types of human and social capital into each other (learning) and into financial capital (working) using the Network Field Model. Now we are ready to describe the exchange of one person's financial capital into another person's financial capital, or *investing*, as indicated in the diagram below (**Figure** 7).

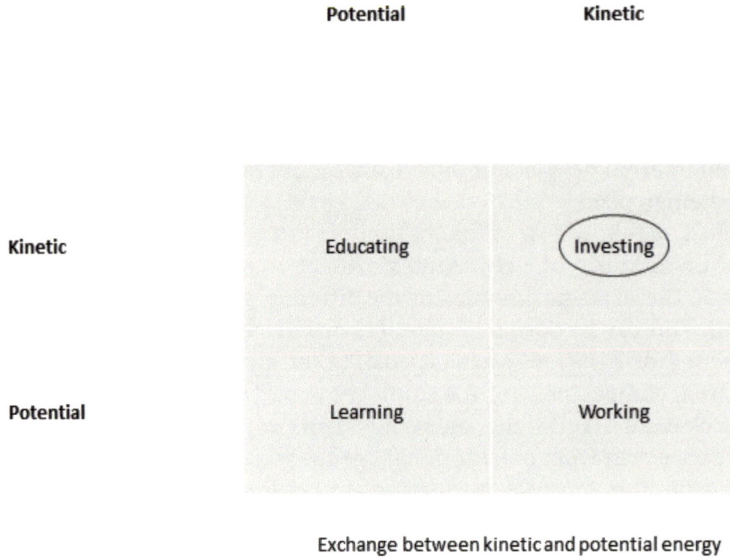

Figure 7.
The Network Field Model—investing.

DOI: http://dx.doi.org/10.5772/intechopen.100574

Maximizing the value of the financial capital means minimizing human and social capital. So when leaders and managers are investing in networks, this strategy should be uppermost in their minds. Will the maximization of financial capital be the overarching strategy? Or is the maximization of human or social capital going to be the strategy? Alternatively, is there a way to achieve a balance between all three types of capital: financial, human and social capital?

We address these questions now.

The value of the financial capital is determined by the appreciation of the assets determined by the market. Any change in the appreciation will be independent of the potential energy. Any changes in the potential energy (e.g., the human and social capital) occur when the object is moving in the network field, *not* by the exchange of financial capital. Movement means a change in r, the relative distance between all the objects in the network. This foundational description reflects the experiences we routinely encounter in society.

Let us explore what we mean by relative distance. Maximizing the contribution of human and social capital occurs at the shortest relative distances or said another way, the network in your neighborhood. Keep in mind that the shortest relative distance is not necessarily grounded in geography. A neighborhood network can be geographically tiny or virtually span the globe. Why? Relative "distance" between two actors in a network is made possible by trust and trust can be achieved over large geographical distances through many asynchronous contacts. This means that financial capital is global and independent of relative position in the field. Investing or exchanging financial capital is solely about earning a return on investment.

According to our diagram, investing means exchanging financial capital. When the exchange takes place inside the network, capital is conserved. However, when financial capital comes from outside the network, the financial capital increases inside the network.

Investing, or the exchange of financial capital, is assumed to have a return on the investment. So, the invested financial capital will be used either to buy the means of production (e.g., those assets necessary to increase production), or to increase human or social capital. This can be done by buying the education (which can be stored in credentialed humans) or buying the social relations, that is, investing in sales power. In this way, the return on the investment is increased.

Apprenticeship and entrepreneurial start-ups are two examples of achieving a return on investment. For example, consider the general statement: educational investments in human capital lead to higher productivity. Higher productivity in turn leads to higher financial capital. These two statements are true.

1. A student might already have the required knowledge, skills and autonomy to do a job, but because he or she was not part of a professional or educational network, the relative distance r is infinite and the value of the social capital is nearly zero. However, we can *invest* using financial capital to decrease the relative distance between "actors" in the network through apprenticeship, thereby increasing social capital. When we put this student inside an apprenticeship or internship network, a relation with the teacher/instructor is created and not only does r become smaller but social capital is created as a function of the developing trust.

2. Entrepreneurial start-ups provide another example. They depend on the trust between the actors as well as the drive to make money with money. Transactions

can only be made when there are links between the actors. We are not investing to make social relations, but rather leveraging social relations to maximize capital: financial, human and/or social.

We define *risk* as the difference between the whole or partial fulfillment of a goal. We define a "gap" as the situation in a network where existing capital is zero for specific circumstances. This has implications for capital. For financial capital, it implies that certain assets, for example, products, are not available for the fulfillment of the goal. For human capital, it implies that the required assets, for example, knowledge, skills and autonomy, are not available. For social capital, it means that required social relations do not exist.

When there is no required capital available, this means that the network is missing a bridge between other networks where the needed human capital may reside. When there is no connection or bridge with possible clients, because the social capital is lacking or deficient, the likelihood that products will be developed is small. Bridges between networks are simply relations of people residing in different networks exhibiting different social capital.

Using the gap concept, we provide a table related to each kind of capital. In the table, we present the purpose of the investment for each type of capital and its associated risk.

	Measuring return	**Possible risk**	**Risk mitigation management**
Financial capital	Measuring the development of the capital as a percentage of the investment	"Gaps" in the product portfolio, so no link to the market allowing for competition	Using client contacts and input in determining the product portfolio
Human capital	Measuring the development of the capabilities and appreciation in the market by means of assessments	"Gaps" in the capabilities make certain goals impossible	Translating assessments of individual network members into a plan for developing capabilities
Social capital	Measurement of the trust in the network using the size of the network and the strength of the connections	"Gaps" in the network disabling contact with clients and partners	Linking different networks including clients and partners

Risk mitigation consists of three steps. The first is determining the purpose of the investment and the underlying strategy. The second is the measurement of the existing capital and possible gaps. The third step is to determine the costs to close the gaps. Then one can decide whether or not to invest in a strategic "project" knowing the risks and related costs involved.

6.1 A scenario for applying the model

Every organization has its own raison d'etre captured explicitly in its strategic goals, financial forecasts and daily decisions. Yet all of these processes are performed by a mixture of the organization's hierarchy, that is, the formal organization of rules and authority and its internal networks, i.e. informal rules and trusted social interactions. When there is a change in strategic direction, there are naturally associated costs. But how can we determine the costs of those changes?

In most cases, senior officers of the organization do not know in any great detail about the talents of the people in the total organization. Neither do Human Resource systems which are largely transactional; providing ages, salary and assessment information and the like. So biased assumptions are generally made about who may not be a good match for executing the new strategy. Similarly, biased assumptions are made about who to hire. For example, making employees redundant in the Netherlands can cost between 3 and 6 months salary, in rough numbers between € 10,000 and € 20,000 EUROS. Hiring new employees in that country costs normally between € 10,000 and € 50,000 EUROS and additionally there is a lag time of 1–3 years to become effective, adding another € 100.000 and € 200.000 to the total cost, which has been indicated by several organizations in the Netherlands we interviewed.

Let us assume you have a company of 10.000 employees and you have a new strategy. HR does an analysis and advises you to fire 1000 people and hire 500 new employees. This would cost you approximately € 1.500.000 firing costs plus € 7.650.000, for the new employees. This change costs you upwards of ten million EUROS.

Another way of accomplishing strategic change is to adopt our model. If your goals are defined, then the new strategy can be profiled describing what skills are necessary to fulfill the goals. Using the model, profiles are made available to all the employees. Using Artificial Intelligence (AI), an optimizing algorithm can be made to match the goals to existing skills and talents in the existing employee pool. The next step is to determine if training is necessary to improve the match between the goal profile and the combined employee network profiles.

After implementing this process, it becomes clear who will still be part of the organization and who will need more training to remain fit for purpose. Assume that instead of firing 1000 employees, only 500 really need to be fired, and instead of hiring 500 new employees, only 250 have to be hired. That means lowering the cost of change from almost 10 million euro to about 5 million euro (including training). The costs of a strategic change are lowered while preserving most of the existing employee base. In fact different scenarios can be made, each using a different set of goals for the existing employee networks. By applying this model one can determine the financial effects of the different scenarios and determine the necessary investments.

Furthermore, return on investment can be monitored over time. Investments in human capital (paying for training and education) and social capital (investing in trust) can be correlated to higher productivity providing a return on financial investment. Unfortunately, most HR assessments are not robustly measuring human or social capital making this measurement untenable under legacy models. However, by using our model, we can make a timeline, match the profiles and measure any changes to production. In this way, investments can be better approximated and monitored.

Therefore, a practical approach for understanding investing is to use profile representations of employee qualifications, for example, an E-portfolio, which incorporates both human and social capital. A “wallet” using blockchain technology tracks the dynamic changes in properties and ownership. We address this more fully in Section 8.

7. Educating

Teacher
let us break
the wall
between what
we can do
together
and what is
wanted
based on some
commercial idea
of the future
organized as a
standard process
of storing information.

Let us
jump
over the line
separating our
possibilities from
what is being
told
and forgotten.

We describe a field as a network consisting of relations between objects. In this field, we describe capital as energy, where every object in the field is characterized by a trifecta of financial, human and social capital. In the previous sections, we explained how humans use integrated information via the network field. We began with learning, then moved on to working and investing. We now tackle educating.

First, we must make a distinction between learning and educating. Both learning and educating are similar in that there is an increase in human capital, knowledge, skills and autonomy and there is an increase in social capital between the objects. The major difference is that educating originates from using financial capital to buy human capital or social capital. So in educating, the human and social capital, originally owned by the actor is valued and then exchanged into financial capital. Essentially it is traded to financial capital. The whole cottage industry of intellectual property rights exists to support and sustain the exchange of human or social capital into a financial transaction.

This is contrasted to learning. Learning is a direct transfer of human or social capital between objects in the network field. There are no intellectual property rights involved. The main difference between education and learning is that the first is based on an economic principle; human and social capital are seen to have economic value and therefore intellectual property rights can be owned by organizations. Whereas in learning, human and social capital is necessary to reach a certain goal and to have a purpose and is free to use by anyone, for example, open source software (**Figure 8**).

In this section we discuss educating as the commercial offering of human and social capital. Our current education system originated from the guild system in the industrial revolution 1.0, where the owners taught others about the craftsmanship and the apprenticeships they owned. The guilds gave way to production demands

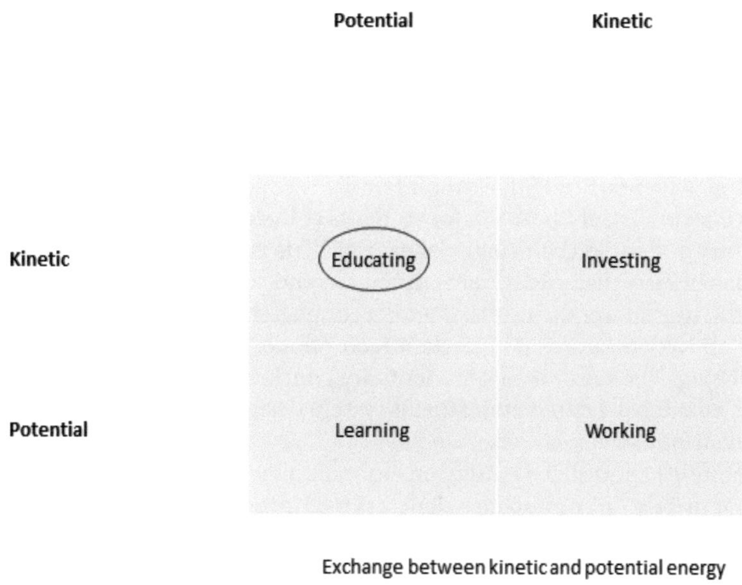

Figure 8.
The Network Field Model—educating.

as the industrial revolution matured and labor became easy and cheap. Some labor still demanded advanced skills like reading and math, so an education system was introduced for children to learn what was needed for work. Education was annually disrupted during harvest season and as knowledge became increasingly standardized, the education academic cycle evolved to K-12 years eventually adding an additional four more years, so that educating was extended into a young adult's life until age 22.

The three disrupters:

Machines and robots: As repetitive tasks become automated and performed by machines, human objects are pushed out of the market into more creative endeavors. Over time, there was less opportunity for them to do repetitive work and a greater need to be engaged in creative activities.

Skills and talents: Financial capital was only invested in activities that have a direct impact on production (according to legacy economic principles). The sole purpose of education was to make you do your job better, not develop your talents.

Living longer: Life expectancy has increased and people are now working longer as a result. Normally the productive cycle was between 20 and 60 years producing a period of career activity of 40 years. Forty years is about the same amount of time as an innovation wave. The uncomfortable irony is that people retire "just in time" as the next innovation wave gets started. So, twentieth century education meant that people were educated to use the new techniques until retirement, just as the next disruption and innovation wave was imminent. This pattern is changing. People are not only living longer, but also capable of working longer because work is increasingly more mental and less physical. The result is an older workforce is merging well into the next innovation wave that will have to be re-educated a second time. So, education was and is episodic when perhaps it should be life-long.

In our model, we describe capital as the combination of financial, human and social capital. The existing education system is established to add human capital. As we referenced earlier, there are only about 15 available years to obtain the enormous amount of knowledge required to get qualified for a job. Still, that leaves unaddressed the social capital side of the equation. What do we do about social capital? This too has been addressed with the relatively new developments in learning such as action learning, Montessori learning and more recently, "personalized" learning.

Remember, the current education system is based on investing in the financial capital of the students. Students or their families are paying for this education. This leads to an enormous debt position for students coinciding with the time they start to earn money and build their financial capital. This is the systems theory model: governments believe that investments in human and social capital are still at the *individual* level. They ignore the fact that work is done in networks and networks build social capital. Networks are an important factor not only in production but also in social wellbeing. The result is that students are continuously investing in developing themselves outside of a dated educational system designed to prepare them to only start (not continue) their careers.

Why shouldn't centralized education embrace a more robust continuous learning strategy, not merely "accommodate" half-hearted attempts to institutionalize and underfund "continuing education" that we see today? A sensible first step in this direction would be to begin with a socializing process whereby tacit knowledge is exchanged in problem-solving goals. This approach is practiced at the graduate level in professional schools such as business or medicine but we suggest that it occurs far too late in the educational process. Student groups can start working together to solve collective problems and reach shared goals. Accessing resources through webinars, literature searches and social networks is critical to development. This is what we define as learning and it is independent of age.

Here is where input from a professor or someone with special knowledge or skills becomes an important step in the overall process of personalized learning. Every individual, each with their own capabilities and talents, should have access to available knowledge and skills. Only when it is clear that the development has reached the desired level, does the moment of internalization arrive, that is, telling the others in the group what has been learned and sharing how it can be used by the group to reach the common goal. This is a learning cycle that is not directed to one's own knowledge, skills and autonomy for a certain job or a set of processes to be performed, but rather it is directed to *optimize* individual talents which can then be used to fulfill a group goal. It represents an entirely different approach.

But the overarching question remains: What should students be learning? A practical solution consists of dividing the incubation time for learning into two segments: (1) beginning at a young age up to about 24 years old (usually funded by taxes) and (2) a public-private partnership where commercial organizations, unions, and governments form curriculum committees to design graduate content. The graduate option is a very cumbersome process that leads in most cases to replicating (and competing) course content between different Institutes of Higher Education (IHEs). Because the schools and universities are competing for funds, these IHEs try to attract more students, failing to update their curriculum - all for the mad rush to meet market demands. The unintended consequence is graduating a generation of students with higher expectations for acquiring jobs but lacking the necessary skills to get jobs. This long cycle has put graduate education further and further behind in creating updated and relevant course content. To put it cynically, students are being trained for jobs that no longer exist. Many graduates believe that the costs of education are simply not worth the money.

The current educational system could accommodate our model with some adjustments. For example, a curriculum for a certain education module is determined by people from the education institute as well as organizations who need this type of trained personnel. This is a public-private partnership. After a meeting of the minds, the economic value is determined and the curriculum is filled with modules containing the needed knowledge transfer. At the end it is measured whether the knowledge transfer has taken place through assessments and accreditation. In this new setup, the curriculum is continuously revised. Students do not pay for the education, rather they pay for the **accreditation**. In this way, people of all ages partake in the curriculum at no cost. The price point occurs when the exam is taken. Paying for access to and then passing the exam certifies that you now have the knowledge.

In summary, first we invest in the social capital in such a way that tacit knowledge can be exchanged and a common goal can be determined. Then we use the result of this social capital investment to exchange knowledge and develop social relations in a process that externalizes the knowledge and skills. Then we invest in human capital to improve our knowledge and skills. Finally, we combine the available knowledge and skills of the individual's network. Only then can we determine the real asset value of the human object. It is the combination of social and human capital that determines this total asset value. Therefore, the application of the Network Field Model results in a match between the total asset value and its appreciation.

8. Using the model in organizing

Profiles
could describe
people but
are just
representations
or even
perceptions of
who they
might be.

People are
real living
beings and
even more
they are able
to love
and share
their feelings.

One could
describe
those as
processes or
even chemical reactions
but how
can I see
my own love for you
my reader
as a perception
or chemical reaction
each moment
we have contact?

In the previous sections, we discussed the different exchange processes in networks and small organizations. The description was based on four quadrants as indicated in given below as a convenience to the reader. In this section, we describe how this model can be used in organizing and optimizing the network.

8.1 Organizing the network

As discussed in Section 2 there are two major aspects in the design of a network: (1) how to organize and (2) what, if any, technology to use. About the first point, we refer to the optimization process for a network to fulfill a specified goal. About the second point, we address the legal aspects for privacy and AI.

How to organize:

In Section 2 we established the inadequacy of twentieth century centralized systems theory and constructed an argument for why a moiety or bifurcated organizational structure should be presumed. For example, a network is a naturally occurring structure and works hand in hand with the hierarchical structure needed to accomplish an organization's goals.

To organize such a type of hybrid network, we need to know the financial, human and social capital of every member of the organization and the goal of the organization. Only when the human and social capital asset is calculated can one sensibly estimate any gaps between the organization's strategy and purpose. Inevitably there will be gaps consisting of missing qualifications, inadequacies and mismatched employees in jobs as we alluded to in Section 7. To organize (and optimize) the network we have to profile the new positions and roles in the network and establish the required qualifications for those positions and roles. Next, we design new processes in the network that can be performed using a mix of the existing human and social capital assets and determining what new assets need to be procured or acquired from outside the organization.

This process of translating a new strategy into organizing the necessary networks is the essence of a decentralized process and can be accomplished much like scenario planning. The way this is done is to make several interations in aligning the human and social asset with the strategic plan in order to ensure financial health. Based on the strategic plan and the overview of all the processes needed to fulfill the purpose of the organization, a network map is drawn where each network has a separate goal to be fulfilled. Only then, can the available human and social capital be distributed and optimized over the networks.

At ground zero, or where a baseline measurement is first made, this estimate is based on only the available capital. Later, one can introduce educating and learning into the optimization process because these efforts are a part of the larger network field. Correlating any changes in the capital is simply incremental re-optimization. For example:

> *We did a longitudinal study in a consultancy firm as part of a PhD project in the Netherlands. This consultancy firm was originally structured in a hierarchical way. Management decided to change to a team structure. Eight teams were formed, focused on water management. The teams were measured on a financial basis i.e. profit and loss. Immediately following the reorganization, we measured the performance of the teams and found two teams performing better and two teams performing poorly than the others. In this instance, we would say there was a normal distribution. The management expected that the teams would learn from the best performing teams resulting in better performance overall due to natural competition. In fact after five years it appeared that all teams were performing almost equally. The poorer performing teams were better and the good teams performed not as well as before. When we investigated the teams as networks including their "bridges", we found that they were built based on personal appreciation ("I knew him/her from previous projects") and that there was no attention given to the "bridges" as conduits of assets between the teams. There was a clear indication of selection bias resulting in a specific age distribution, i.e., teams with older members and teams with younger members. Teams did not sort themselves based on qualifications. After seven years, the team structure was abandoned in favor of a new reorganization.*

The problem with relying only on leadership is that there are different types of leadership and different types of teams. When analyzed from a point of view of systems theory, mismatches occur. As you can guess, optimization of a team based on the Network Field Model, means that knowing the whole team's qualifications profile will give better results.

8.2 The evolving role of technology

In the twentieth century in the two decades spanning 1970–1990, financial capital started an innovation wave based on information technology. Chips, networking, computing all added up to a new way of producing goods and services. Society was largely centralized using an administrative workforce augmented with computers, factory workers and robots.

An innovation wave began in the twenty-first century, pivoting away from the twentieth century approach and instead focusing on *how* people work, not "what" they worked on. Knowledge was collectivized in collaborative, smaller and nimbler networks where no one person owned an idea; rather ideas were collaboratively conceived and shared with others. People used social media to support and expand their collaborative connections. This is what we came to recognize as a social capital-based society where work is not an individual activity but group or network-based processes. Capabilities are exchanged through shared connections between the actors in the group. These shared connections are held in place not by the authority predicated by the hierarchy but rather through trust-based relationships in the network, accelerated in part by social media platforms. This evolving decentralized social structure may also include a decentralized system for the economy (e.g., basic income), a decentralized system for matching talents, capabilities and work (e.g., individual E-portfolio's) and a decentralized system for education (e.g., personalized learning).

This twenty-first century advancement is in fact another industrial revolution, a version 2.0 if you will, steering away from financially supported human capital in centralized distribution systems to financially supported social capital in decentralized networks. In the latter, two qualities of the actors are leveraged: human capital AND social capital. In these decentralized systems, the value of connections and the role of trust become paramount. The implementation of these decentralized systems will be slow. Look at how long it has taken for peer-to-peer systems to be adopted in the corporate workforce. Slow adoption rates are due in part to battling with legacy systems. This is the slow part of the innovation wave. But we believe this is due to change very soon.

Legacy ownership (e.g., financial capital), is centralized and because it is centralized, it produces frictional drag when attempting to implement a decentralized system. For example, in a financial capital-based society, ownership lies with the one who pays or the one who is using the financial capital to invest. So, ownership of this system is transferred from the creator to the investor. The properties of a person are owned and can include facial recognition, health records, knowledge, skills and social networks. This view of centralized ownership is grim and dystopian.

In contrast, in decentralized systems, all the data related to the properties of individuals belong to the individual. The properties are used for labor and the labor is sold to the investor at the economic value. But an additional value is created in decentralized systems. The properties of an individual are exponentially multiplied because this person is embedded in knowledge networks, teams or small groups. Therefore, in a decentralized model, we have to consider not only the financial capital and the way knowledge and skills are used for the labor, but we also have to consider the total capital in groups and the properties of the individuals in the group performing the work.

We have proposed a hybrid organizational structure and technology where the network is combined with the hierarchical organization. This means a centralized system for control and a decentralized system leveraging personal data (see **Figure 9**). For example, we have solutions running on a central application (running in the cloud) plus decentralized systems (running on the smartphone) to support the individual

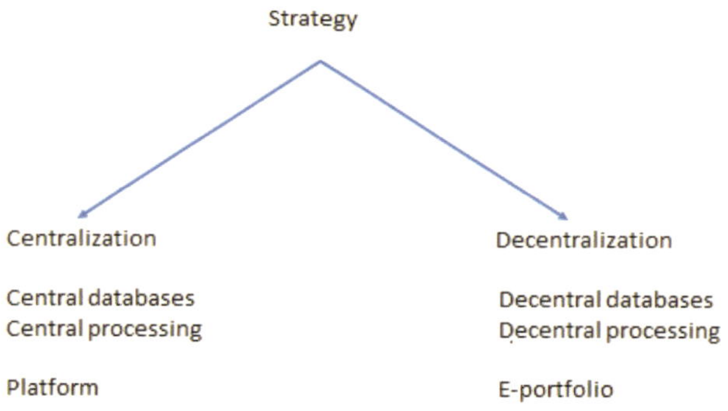

Figure 9.
Strategic organizing.

client or employee linked to the organization. This hybrid technical architecture has some special problems or pitfalls.

The first problem is privacy. Since financial, human and social capital represent properties of an individual, they are considered personal data, and General Data Protection Regulation (GDPR) must be applied. This means that only the individual can access his or her personal information and can give approval for the exchange of their personal data with other applications.

The second problem is institutional supervision or audit. At the moment several organizations, such as banks, insurance companies, health care organizations and others supervise or audit our data. Because possible fraud or misuse of the data is a distinct possibility, a decentralized blockchain protecting private data solves this problem nicely. Blockchain is based on the idea that not only the individual data is stored in a way that only the owner can give permission to use but also that the transactions, the exchange of data, is encrypted and stored in a way that they cannot be manipulated.

It is important to mention that the data stored in such a personal database are time-dependent which means they can be updated every time something changes. This could be the case when an exam is completed and graded, a job change, extra work or a new hobby, change in the network or just new information about personal behavior form a regular update. This is very important from the standpoint of research because a timeline can demonstrate evolving developments in financial, human and social capital about changes in the marketplace as well as in the networks in which one is embedded. It also means that any changes in human capital can be monitored to measure the educating process itself. Currently, this is quite difficult because there is no effective alumni network in decentralized education. The closest approximations to an alumni network are professional networks documented on LinkedIn or similar platforms.

In summary, we propose that this hybrid system consists of both a centralized and decentralized approach. We have previously referred to the decentralized portion as an E-portfolio. An E-portfolio stores all personal individual data as well as all the transactions related to the exchange of financial and potential energy. We assert that this aggregation of individual human properties, secured through the digital signature of its creator, is far superior and more secure than the centralized state-run systems like the Chinese social credit score.

9. Conclusions

Our whole
life
consists of
to know
and
to do.

We learn
from others
the colours
how to speak
and behave
accordingly.

We train
ourselves to
eat properly
use our hands
to caress.

Then comes this
moment of
independency
living on
yourself with
new relations
applying everything
you learned
to earn
new trust
and new money.

Until you look
into the eyes
of your children
and see what
they need
to know.

When we began this project, we investigated "teamwork" and found that research focused mostly on the individual object in the team. Systems theory was used to describe the effects of the input from the environment on the processes, which impacted the object, and then led to results as output. Systems theory does not address the synchronous influence of different objects on each other; it only describes the processes of each object independently of each other.

To solve the bidirectional influence of objects on each other we proposed using the Network Field Model to describe the role of actors in a network working together. This is based on the mathematical description of a Lagrange for a field. Our approach is synchronized with other field approaches: for example, we know we can calculate the effect of each object in the gravitational or electromagnetic field and likewise, we can calculate the effect of human objects in the network field. Field theory always uses two types of energy to describe the value of the field at a certain position and time, kinetic and potential energy. By analogy we use kinetic energy and potential energy in the Network Field Model, where the value of the kinetic energy is the value of the financial capital, the value of the assets, and the value of the potential energy consists of human capital, the value of the knowledge, skills and autonomy, and the social capital, the value of the relations in the team or the network.

To accurately capture the "influence" of actors on each other, especially in the case of the exchange of potential energy, we introduce the concepts of appreciation and trust. We use the term "appreciation" to describe the difference in the value of the representation of the potential energy. We use the term "trust" to describe the weight factor for the exchange of potential energy. We apply the rules for least action and conservation of energy, or capital, in a closed system.

Our model of the network field explains what happens when changes are made in the field. This is important from an economic, sociological and psychological viewpoint. We not only want to know the effect of investments, such as adding capital, to networks, say for example when you are trying to determine the strategy of the organization, but also the effect of the changes on the properties of the objects as it pertains to their ability to fulfill a goal. Our model allows for different scenarios to be imagined for different networks in the organization making it possible to make optimized strategic decisions. It also allows each individual to look for matching opportunities based on existing or future qualifications. Since our model uses qualifications as a representation of the human and social capital and no personal information like age, gender or background, the matching process contains no implicit bias.

It is important to use a standard set of qualifications. We use in our model the European Qualification Framework (EQF). In this framework, one can describe the individual qualifications as well as the qualifications needed for a job and the change to qualifications as a result of learning or education.

We described the results of the application of the model in four different scenarios related to the exchange of energy. We showed that exchanging the potential energy of one person into the potential energy of another person can be interpreted as a socialization process or learning. When kinetic energy is exchanged into potential energy, we describe this as educating. Educating is a centralized process directed at maximizing the return on investment. Hence education and learning are very different types of activities in the field.

We use the term *working* to describe the exchange of potential energy into kinetic energy. We have shown that when using a strictly financial approach, that is, maximizing the return on the investment, will lead to a mismatch between (job) demand and qualifications. This corresponds with the Job Demand-Resource model (JDR), developed to explain burn-out situations for individual workers. Our field model correctly diagnoses burn-out as a result of resource gaps as well as potentially optimizing resource matching to produce flow.

Another result of the application of the model is the impact of strategy on the whole organization. Currently, it is almost impossible to calculate the financial effects of those changes because of the lack of an appropriate model to translate between new goals and the qualifications needed to meet those new goals. Current HR systems are mostly salary and function-oriented and do not give information about qualifications. By representing the human and social capital of the employees and the goals into qualifications one can calculate scenarios for building new networks optimized for the goals including when training is necessary. In this way, the financial consequences of the strategic decision can be calculated in advance of implementation.

Perhaps the most important application of the model is the support of lifelong learning. We learn during our whole life to cope with all the changes innovation brings us. Everyone, including young and old students should have the possibility to search (on demand) how their qualifications fit with the (new) demands and how learning and educating can help to make the best fit. Using algorithms and a qualification system, it is easier to match personal qualifications with opportunities. In this way, it is possible to measure changes over time, that is, the efficacy of both learning and educating.

We have translated the model into different algorithms to be used for the matching of the individual qualifications with (possible) jobs in networks. This is done using artificial intelligence for the optimization process as described in the appendix "Mathematical description of the Network Field Model". Using the optimization process, recruitment or reorganizing networks can be done rapidly without implicit bias.

In volume two we show the reader how to use the model for organizing by optimizing teams to reach specified goals. One can also calculate the effect on those teams when goals and/or team memberships are changed. This is a major advantage over other models because it allows you to develop *measurable* scenarios. You can then calculate with greater precision the consequences of those scenarios for any organization or team.

Glossary

1. The "network field" is a network of objects in a scalar field; each object in the field is influenced by all the other objects in the field.

2. We use a scalar function to describe the field, that is, the function will have a real value at each point in the field.

3. The field is infinite and influences the objects depending on their properties and their relative distance.

4. The field can be described by a Lagrangian, L. The Lagrangian will have a Kinetic energy and Potential energy part:

$$L = \text{Kinetic Energy} - \text{Potential Energy}$$

   - Potential Energy is defined by the Human Capital and Social Capital.

   - Kinetic Energy is defined by the Financial Capital.

5. The Socion is a construct describing what energy is exchanged in the field. It is dependent on the properties and the relative distance of the objects in the field.

6. Organizing is the process of ongoing mutual or reciprocal influence on the objects in the field.

7. An organization is the result of organizing at a certain point in time. As a result of the process of organizing, nonrandom structures can arise including markets, hierarchies, networks and heterarchies.

   - A market is a special case where the exchange process is influenced using non-repetitive transactions, for example, exchanges.

   - A hierarchy is a special case where the exchange process is influenced using authoritative and coercive power.

   - A network is a special case where the exchange process is influenced using repetitive mutual relations.

   - A heterarchy is a special case where the exchange process is influenced using collaborative and intermittent exchanges.

8. A team is a subset of an organization, authorized by the organization, and has the properties of a network.

9. Value is the result of a measurement of the available capital according to an objective valuation scheme.

10. Appreciated value is the subjective value given by an individual to an amount of capital needed or wanted.

11. The Capital of an object is a general term consisting of the available energy to be applied for the fulfillment of a certain goal.

    - Financial Capital is defined as the value of the assets. Financial capital is represented by the economic value in a chosen currency of the assets owned by the object (in most cases a human object).

    - Human Capital is defined as the value of the available knowledge, skills and autonomy of the object (in most cases a human actor) and is represented by a matrix S containing the properties of the object.

    - Social Capital is defined as the value of the available relations with other objects (in most scases a human object) in the network. Specifically, social capital is represented by the trust between two objects.

12. The properties of an object are defined by three factors:

    - the representation of the assets owned.

    - the representation of the existing knowledge, skills and autonomy.

    - the representation of the existing relations measured by the links consisting of (a)symmetric communications with other objects in the field.

13. Communication is the act of exchanging information by speaking, writing, or using some other medium.

14. Influence is the act of having an effect on the properties, development, or behavior of an object.

15. Trust is the frequency of applying influence and it is used as a weight factor for the exchange of energy.

16. Disclaimer: The term “object” is an amalgam, derived from two sources: (1) from the term “element” originating in the natural science literature, (2) from the term “actor” originating from the humanities literature.

DOI: http://dx.doi.org/10.5772/intechopen.100574

Acknowledgements

In writing this book together, we each came from different directions, halfway around the world yet always working on the same ideas ("spooky at a distance" to borrow from Einstein). Many people and institutions influenced us. Special thanks should be given to those who occupy the academic institutions of The Hague University of Applied Sciences, Erasmus University in Rotterdam, Yale University and Harvard University. They constructively got out of the way because of our enthusiasm or put obstacles in the path despite our enthusiasm. Either way, they sharpened our thinking and made us stronger.

Special recognition goes to the reviewers of our manuscript. Their input and suggestions refined our language and logic. We wish to thank Ian James, Jeanne and Barry Frew, and the editors at IntechOpen.

This book is dedicated to Richard Feynman.

Suggested reading

Ethnographies about the impact of networks can be read in Tom Allen's Managing the Flow of Technology (Cambridge, MA: The MIT Press, 1977) and J. A. Barnes, Social Networks (Addison-Wesley Modular Publishing, 1972, 26, 1-29). For a great story about how anthropologists were duped by the social networks of their informants, read W. H. R. Rivers, Kinship and Social Organization (New York: Humanities Press, 1968). Another classic is Bailey's Stratagems and Spoils: A Social Anthropology of Politics (Oxford: Basil Blackwell, 1969).

Conceptual efforts to categorize networks can be found in Barabasi's 2002 book Linked: The New Science of Networks (Perseus Publishing). An earlier approach can be found in Jeremy Boissevain's 1974 Friends of Friends (Oxford: Basil Blackwell). An early trendsetter can be read in Walter Powell's "Neither Market Nor Hierarchy: Network Forms of Organization," Organizational Behavior, 1990, 12, 295-336. A small classic is Duncan Watts's Small Worlds (Princeton University Press, 1999). The yin and yang of connection through two opposing forces of heterarchy and hierarchy can be read in Stephenson's 2009 article on heterarchy, entitled "Neither Hierarchy nor Network" in People and Strategy, 31, 4, 4-13.

The highs and lows of hierarchy are discussed in Charles Bosk, Forgive and Remember: Managing Medical Failure (Chicago: University of Chicago Press, 1978). Two insightful approaches into hierarchy can be read in Pierre Bourdieu's Distinction (Cambridge University Press, 1984) and Homo Academicus (Stanford University Press, 1988). Also take a look at Mary Douglas's series of Princeton lectures in How Institutions Think (Syracuse: Syracuse University Press, 1986). An insightful rendition can be found in Louis Dumont's Homo Hierarchicus (Chicago: University of Chicago Press, 1952) and Jaques Elliott's 1990 "In Praise of Hierarchy," Harvard Business Review, 127-133. Great insights can also be found in Marshall Sahlins' "The Segmentary Lineage: An Organization for Predatory Expansion," American Anthropologist, 1961, 63, 322-345, and "Poor Man, Rich Man, Big Man, Chief: Political Types in Melanesia and Polynesia," Comparative Studies in Society and History, 1963, 5, 285-303.

Technical aspects of network measures including articles on centrality can be found in Hage and Harary's 1983 book entitled Structural Models in Anthropology (New York: Cambridge University Press). Following later was Ron Burt's Structural Holes, (Cambridge, MA: Harvard University Press, 1992). A good read is D. Brass's "Being in the Right Place: A Structural Analysis of Individual Influence in an Organization", Administrative Science Quarterly, 1984, 29(4), 518-539. A "reviewed" review on centrality can be found in Linton Freeman's "A Set of Measures of Centrality Based on Betweenness," Sociometry, 1977, 40, 35-41, and his 1979 work "Centrality in Social Networks I: Conceptual Clarification," Social Networks 1, 215-239. A review of that review can be found in Stephenson and Zelen's "Rethinking Centrality," Social Networks, 1989, 1, 1-37. See also D. Koehn's "Should We Trust Trust?" in American Business Law Journal, 1996, 34(2), 184-203. The link to social field and social capital is given by Mathieu Hilgers and Eric Mangez, Bourdieu's Theory of Social Fields, ISBN978-1-138-92104-7,Routledge New York 2015 and David Halpern, Social Capital, ISBN 978-0-7456-2548-5, Polity Press, 1988 or Nicholas Christakis & James Fowler, Connected, ISBN 978-0-00-730360-1, Harper Press, 2011. On the other hand the link to flow and productivity can be found in Tjip de Jong, Linking Social Capital to knowledge productivity, ISBN 978-90-313-8209-5, Springer Uitgeverij, 2010.

How networks congeal and create boundaries and barriers to entry can be read in Fredrik Barth's complete work entitled Ethnic Groups and Boundaries (Boston:

Little, Brown and Company, 1969). A more technical reading can be found in E. J. Bienenstock, P. Bonacich, and M. Oliver's 1990 work "The Effect of Network Density and Homogeneity on Attitude Polarization," Social Networks, 12, 153-172 as well as E. J. Bienenstock, and P. Bonacich's 1992 article entitled "The Core as a Solution to Exclusionary Networks," Social Networks, 4, 231-243. One way to understand boundaries is to understand how they are breached. Read Malcolm Gladwell's, The Tipping Point (Boston: Little, Brown and Company, 2000). A classic read on contagion is E. Rogers work on the Diffusion of Innovations (New York: The Free Press, 1963).

The best philosophical discussions of networks without directly talking about networks can be found in Samual B. Griffith 6th Cent B C Sun-Tzu, The Art of War, Oxford University Press, 1963 as well as one of my favorite authors in the 1961 edition of Niccolo Machiavelli, The Prince, trans. George Bull (New York: Penguin). Closely related to Machiavelli's insights is the work of Michel Foucault, in particular, the 1979 edition of Discipline and Punish (New York: Vintage Books) and the 1970 edition of The Order of Things by the same publisher. Durkheim provides wonderful insights into networks in The Division of Labor in Society (1933: New York: The Free Press, 1933). An excellent read can be found in A. Gouldner "The Norm of Reciprocity: A Preliminary Statement," American Sociological Review, 1960, 25, 161-178. Another classic is R. Axelrod's The Complexity of Cooperation (Princeton University Press, 1997). A seminal article is Mark Granovetter's "Economic Action and Social Structure: The Problem of Embeddedness," American Journal of Sociology, 91(3), 481-510, as well as his more popular, but less theoretical "The Strength of Weak Ties," American Journal of Sociology, 1973, 78, 1360-1380.

Writing about employee engagement can be found in Stephenson's "Building a Culture of Trust" in Employee Engagement: Building High- Performance People and Organizations, edited by Martha Finney (Praeger-Greenwood, 2008, 123-135). The dilemma related to work and jobs are beautifully presented in David Graeber, Bullshit jobs, EAN 9780241267363, Penguin, 2018. Robert M. Solow, Learning from learning by doing, EAN 9780804728416, Stanford University Press, 1997 is more directed to the learning process itself. The problem of organizing has many aspects which can be described in different ways. When looking from the point of view of the process of organizing Peter Peverelli & Karen Verduyn, Understanding the basic dynamics of organizing, ISBN 978-90-5972-686-4, Eburon Academic Publishers, 2012 give a good background. In case of the building of network organizations at the very beginning the contribution of S.C.A. Peters and R. Frisart, Network Organisations, ISBN 90-5590-044-3, Lansa Publishing, 2000 can help. The possible effects of a mismatch between job demand and the qualifications is described in Schaufeli, W.B. & Bakker A.B. (2004), Job demands, job resources and their relation with burnout and engagement: A multi sample study. Journal of Organizational Behavior, 25, 293-315.

We use algorithms in our data analysis in much the same way as it is being used in physics ((see Alex Pentland. in Social Physics, ISBN 978-1-59420-565-1, The Penguin Press, 2014). To learn more about the physics and how field theory was developed, we suggest starting with Schrödinger, What is Life ISBN 978-1-107-60466-7, Cambridge University Press 1967 and Carl Friedrich Weizsäcker, Die Einheit der Natur, ISBN 3-446-12743-7, Carl Hanser Verslag München Wien 1971. The basics of field theory can be found in the physics series made by Leonard Susskind and Art Friedman. Also Michio Kaku, Physics of the future, ISBN 978-0-141-04424-8, Penguin books, 2011, and Robert Gavin Alexander, The Leibniz Clark correspondence, ISBN 978-0-719-00669-2, Manchester University Press, 1977 give a good background.

References

[1] Karl E. Weick, Making Sense of the Organization. New Yersey: Blackwell Publishers; 2001

[2] Foucault. The Order of Things. New York: Vintage Books; 1970

[3] Levi-Strauss. The mathematics of man. Social Science Bulletin. 1955;**6**:581-590

[4] Susskind L, Friedman A. Special Relativity and Classical Field Theory. London: Penguin Books; 2017

[5] Feynman, Sands, Leighton. Feynman Lectures on Physics. New York: Basic Book; 2011

[6] Mauss. The Gift (Trans). New York: Norton; 1950

[7] Bourdieu. Distinction. Cambridge or Oxon: Cambridge University Press; 1984

[8] Csikszentmihalyi M. Flow. New York: Harper Row; 1990

[9] Nonaka I, Takeuchi H. The Knowledge Creating Company: How Japanese Companies Create the Dynamics of Innovation. New York: Oxford University Press; 1995

[10] Bourdieu. Cambridge: The Logic of Practice. Stanford University Press; 1990

[11] Gratton L, Scott A, editors. The 100 Year Life. London: Bloomsbury Information; 2016

[12] Christensen CM. The Innovator's Dilemma. Harvard Business Review Press; 2016

Author details

Steef Peters[1] and Karen Stephenson[2*]

1 The Hague University of Applied Sciences, The Netherlands

2 The Erasmus University Rotterdam, The Netherlands

*Address all correspondence to: karenor182@gmail.com

Chapter

Mathematical Description of the Network Field Model

Steve Peters and Karen Stephenson

Abstract

In this addendum, which was the basis for an article published at the network conference 2021, we discuss a mathematical description of a network field. We describe the exchange of capital between objects in a team which we call a network. We make the assumption that exchanging capital between the actors in the field is the same as exchanging kinetic and potential energy. In our model, we use three types of capital: financial, human, and social to represent the qualifications of an object. By analogy, a non-relativistic gravitational field can be described by a time dependent *Kinetic Energy* part minus a position-dependent *Potential Energy* part. Here we describe a non-relativistic network field as Lagrangian with a time-dependent *Financial Capital* part minus a relative position-dependent *Potential energy* part. The description of the network field and especially the potential energy for a certain area in the field is comparable to the description of a Graph Neural Network for a set of nodes, a concept from deep learning theory. We use the Graph Neural Network to analyze the effects of exchanging potential energy in a network. We also use it to calculate the optimum distribution of qualifications of the actors in a team.

Keywords: network field, optimizing teams, artificial intelligence, graph neural network

1. Introduction

In our model, we use the definition of a network field comparable to a gravitational or electromagnetic field in a closed system. We use a scalar field describing the distribution of the total capital using a Lagrangian, so the field has a real value at each point in four-dimensional spacetime. We assume that an object in a network can be seen as a point-like object in the field. The field is defined as $\varphi(X_\mu)$, where X_μ defines the position in the μ-dimensional space. In this case, we have a four-dimensional spacetime with the coordinates $X_\mu = t, r, \theta, \zeta$. The position at a certain time t is defined by r, θ, ζ. It is relative to the node in the network considered where r, the relative distance, is the path length between the objects in the network.

The total capital of an object consists of financial, human, and social capital. The value of the financial capital, $F_{capital}$, is defined as the total value of the tangible assets, an object owns as appreciated by the market. It is time-dependent because its value changes in time. The value is measured according to the economic principles for valuing tangible assets.

The value of the human capital, $H_{capital}$, is defined as the value of the knowledge, skills, and autonomy. The value is measured by using the European Qualification Framework (EQF).

The value of the social capital, $S_{capital}$, is determined by the trust in the relations of an object with other objects in the network. This relation is given by the density of the capital exchange, the sum of the links, between the objects. The value of the social capital is measured by the frequency of contact between two objects.

The total capital in the network as a closed system is constant

$$Total_{capital} = F_{capital} + \left(H_{capital} * S_{capital}\right). \tag{1}$$

The Lagrangian to describe the network field is then

$$L = F_{capital} - \left(H_{capital} * S_{capital}\right) \tag{2}$$

$F_{capital}$ can be described as the kinetic energy in the classical mechanic sense, where defining the value of the financial capital at $t = 0$ and the speed as an increase of the capital as a function of time

$$F_{capital}(t) = F_{capital}(t=0) * \left(1 + ROI(t)\right) \tag{3}$$

where $ROI(t)$ is the return of investment on the financial capital in time or

$$ROI(t) = dF_{capital}(t) / dt. \tag{4}$$

We can represent the human capital of object i in a matrix Q_i, where the columns in the matrix are the representation of the amount of knowledge, skills, and autonomy. The rows are determined by the area of knowledge, skills, and autonomy. We represent the social capital as the trust matrix T, where T_{ij} describes the trust between objects i and j, and T_i is the sum for the trust of node i over all other nodes j in the network.

We can then define the value of the potential energy $V_i(\Phi)$ for an object i in our coordination system as

$$V_i(\Phi) = \int\int\int\left(T_i * \left(Q_j - Q_i\right) / r^2\right) dr d\theta d\zeta \tag{5}$$

so the Lagrangian becomes

$$L = F_{capital}(t=0) * \left(1 + ROI(t)\right) - \int\int\int\left(T_i * \left(Q_j - Q_i\right) / r^2\right) dr d\theta d\zeta. \tag{6}$$

In our graph representation, the financial capital stays the same, because the graph representation is at a certain time t. The Lagrangian in the graph representation shows only the potential energy part, where we do not integrate over the angles θ and ζ

$$V_i(\Phi) = \sum_j T_{ij} * \left(Q_j - Q_i\right) / r^2 \tag{7}$$

2. Applying the network field model

The main purpose of the Network Field Model is to describe the exchange of energy, *capital*, between objects in a network or team in order to fulfill a certain goal. This will allow us to find an optimum for a set of objects to form a network or a team. We do not take the internal structure of the objects into consideration. We only use a representation of the properties of the objects in the matrices Q and T as a result of learning and behavior in the past. We assume that the field and the total capital in the network stay the same at a certain time t independent of changes in positions of the objects in the field. The energy distribution in the field can, however, change in time. In that case (and based on the least action rule) there will be only a change in the time-dependent part of the Lagrangian of the actors, the financial capital.

To optimize a network or a team by using the representations of the objects, one has to also use a representation of the goal of the team and assume that the goal can be fulfilled by a finite amount of objects in the team. The first step is to use the representations as a fixed value, especially the trust. Secondly one could further optimize the team by using trust as a weight factor that could be changed within certain limits. In this way, one is using a graph representation of the team and optimizes the distribution of the given representations of the individual objects for the goal. A further step would be to change the values of the individual objects by introducing learning. This is described in more detail below.

3. Using the model for deep learning

In the Network Field Model, we assume that the objects are point-like objects with certain properties where the properties determine the coupling to the field (one could assume that humans are intelligent beings able to process information; therefore, their properties could change without coupling to the field). However, in our description, we assume that all the information needed for a change in properties is a result of the coupling to the field. One of these changes could be the result of learning, the exchange of potential (human and social) capital between two actors.

The description of the field and especially the potential energy as given in (5) for a certain area $dr d\theta d\zeta$ in space or as given in (7) when we only consider the relations between the nodes. This is comparable to the description of a graph neural network (GNN) where the iteration function for the neuron or node is described as

$$f(x_i) := \varphi\left\{\sum_1^n x(i) * w(i)\right\} \quad (8)$$

where $x(i)$ describes the classification of node i and $w(i)$ the weight factor. In our model, the function used is $(Q_j - Q_i)/r^2$ and the weight matrix T_{ij}.

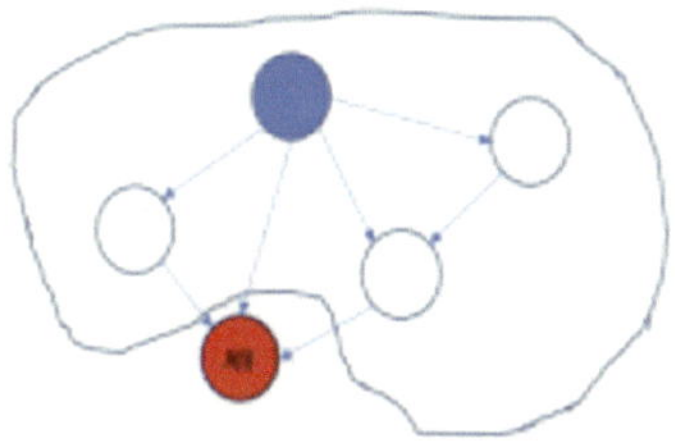

The properties of the object or node i are described by the matrix Q_i.

The purpose is to determine the properties of node i in relation to the other nodes. In other words, one can determine the fit of that node in the network. This can be done by using deep learning for the graph network. For the iteration process, one can state that

$$M_i^{(k)} = g\left(M_i^{(k-1)}, \sum_j h\left(Q_i^{(k-1)}\right)\right) \quad (9)$$

where $h(M_i) = T_{ij} * (Q_j - Q_i) / r^2$ is the iteration and g the iteration function.

4. Conclusion

In this article, we have presented a model for a network field for objects in a network. In the model, we use three types of capital: financial, human, and social. We are able to determine the effects of changes in the different types of capital, like financial investments, education, or the building of new relations. The impact of change on teams or networks and the role of the objects in the teams or networks can be calculated by using the deep learning technique.

Author details

Steve Peters[1] and Karen Stephenson[2*]

1 The Hague University of Applied Sciences, The Hague, Netherlands

2 Erasmus University Rotterdam, Rotterdam, Netherlands

*Address all correspondence to: karenor182@gmail.com